Search and Rescue Dogs: Training the K-9 Hero

2nd Edition

American Rescue Dog Association

Howell Book House

HOWELL
BOOK
HOUSE

Wiley Publishing, Inc.

For general information about our other products and services, please contact our Customer Care Department within the United States at (800) 762-2974, outside the United States at (317) 572-3993 or fax (317) 572-4002.

Wiley also publishes its books in a variety of electronic formats. Some content that appears in print may not be available in electronic books. For more information about Wiley products, visit our web site at www.wiley.com.

Library of Congress Cataloging-in-Publication Data
Search and rescue dogs : training the k-9 hero.— 2nd ed.
    p. cm.
Includes index.
ISBN 978-0-7645-6703-2
 1. Search dogs—Training. 2. Rescue dogs—Training. I. Howell Book House.
 SF428.73 .S43 2002
 636.7'0886—dc21
                              2002009303
Manufactured in the United States of America
10 9 8 7

Second Edition

Book design by Marie Kristine Parial-Leonardo
Cover design by Susan Olinsky
Front cover photo: Police Officer David Sanabria and K-9 Storm in front of the Marriot Vista Hotel, Ground Zero. *Photo: Lt. Daniel Donadio, NYPD K-9*

This book is dedicated to:
The memory of Bill Syrotuck;
Jean Syrotuck Whittle;
the handlers and support personnel who have contributed
so much to the
American Rescue Dog Association;
and to the dogs, without whom none of this would have been possible

Contents

— Acknowledgments —

The American Rescue Dog Association (ARDA) wishes to express deep appreciation to Jean Syrotuck Whittle, upon whose pioneering field research and original diagrams much of this book is based.

Special recognition must go to Alice Stanley (Virginia Unit) for her original contributions, as well as for compiling and editing the entire manuscript.

The following ARDA unit members made significant contributions to the manuscript: Penny and Tim Sullivan, Emil Pelcak, Heidi Ludewig, Sue Lavoie, Tom Connors and James Pearson (New Jersey Unit); Garrett Dyer, Sonja Heritage, Elizabeth Kreitler and Gamble McCown (Maryland Unit); Tony Campion (Wisconsin Unit); and Doug Stanley (Virginia Unit).

We would also like to thank Sherri Gallagher (Illinois Unit); Jane Adair (Virginia Unit); Vicki and Chuck Wooters and Roseann Keller (Pennsylvania Unit); Doug Teeft (Nova Scotia Unit); and Charles Keuhn and Dean Goulet (Wisconsin Unit).

In addition, we wish to thank the following: Linda Warshaw, who provided most of the artwork; Jeff Doran, Dick Schusler and Larry Hinkle (Washington Unit); Bob and Marcia Koenig (Texas Unit); Don Arner (New York Unit); Bev Niehaus (Wisconsin Unit); Bill Squire (New Mexico Unit); the veterinarians who reviewed the chapter on first aid for search dogs: Bruce A. Beckman, Douglas L. Moldoff, David Herrick and Dan Parkinson; the River Vale, New Jersey, Police Department; Lieutenant Daniel Donadio of the New York City Emergency Services Unit K-9 Team; and Trooper Michael W. Berry, Virginia State Police Dive Team Coordinator, PADI Master Scuba Diver Trainer.

Much of the material in Chapters 4, 5 and 6 is from Bill Syrotuck's *Training Steps for Search and Rescue Dogs*, written in 1974. Bill died before he could polish the manuscript and, with the kind assistance of Jean Syrotuck Whittle and Don Arner, former publisher of *Off Lead* magazine, we have done so for this book.

The majority of material contained in Chapters 8 and 9 is from Bill Syrotuck's pamphlet *The Search and Rescue Dog Unit, Part 1* written in 1969.

Foreword

Before and after. All our lives are now forever divided into two segments—*before* September 11th, and *after.*

Before that date, when we heard the term "search-and-rescue dog," we thought of a little boy lost in the woods, or perhaps an avalanche victim, or a hiker lost on a cold night. But those perceptions were *before.*

September 11th catapulted search dogs—and their intrepid handlers—to the forefront of our consciousness and placed them in a new setting of twisted metal and choking dust. In those still-hopeful days immediately after the tragedy, the dogs became a clear symbol of our hope and our determination. Most of us heard the stories about how, when the rescue workers heard the call, "Dog coming through," the crowds parted instantly to let them pass. Universally, we knew they were our first line of hope in finding anyone still alive.

What most of us did not hear were the stories about how the dogs comforted the workers, especially the firemen, some of whom could express their overwhelming grief and confide their waning hope only to the quiet acceptance of a dog. These oh-so-special dogs not only devote their unique talents to working for us in our time of need—in the worst of conditions—but are also so much more than willing to provide therapy for us, too.

These dogs give all they can, and ask for next to nothing in return. They don't want more days off, or paid sick days, or cushy working conditions, or even a guaranteed retirement benefit. They are pleased to give their all for us, and happy just to receive our gratitude.

When the teams were honored five months later at the Westminster Kennel Club Dog Show, thousands watched the televised ceremony and wept, once again, tears of gratitude, and remembrance, and sadness. We knew there was no honor great enough to bestow upon them. And we would, quite simply, never think of them in the same way again—*after.*

This book is the same. The *before* book was already a complete and useful manual on how to train an efficient search and rescue dog. But this revised, *after* edition, clearly reflects the changes. I suspect many will pick up this book now just to read the chilling, but mesmerizing, accounts of the search dog work at the Oklahoma City bombing disaster and the earthquakes abroad, as well as at the World Trade Center tragedy.

Before, the search dog teams were often called in many hours, or even days, after other methods had failed, as several of the stories in the original edition recount. Thankfully, the new attitude is to call the dog-handler teams in first, when there is the most hope of them being successful.

The new and expanded chapters bring this book up-to-date with what is expected of search dogs and handlers today, and what may be required of them in the future. This book is now not only a training manual, it is a fitting tribute to the dogs and handlers who serve on the front lines of our modern-day battlefields, at home and abroad, wherever they are called. Besides its clear presentation of excellent training principles and exercises, and a healthy dose of just plain common sense, this book also covers everything from puppy selection and first aid, to tactical deployment, weather and equipment, along with extensive handler training.

In the hours and days directly after September 11th, everyone wanted to help in some way. But, as this book clearly outlines, a search and rescue team is a unique unit. A certain kind of handler and a very special dog are bonded together through arduous and complex training that takes them far beyond any capabilities that they would have had individually.

Prepare to enter the world of canine communication and handler savvy that combine to produce the teams we now depend on more than ever. This was a good book *before*. It is even more important today—*after*.

Sheila Booth

Sheila Booth is the author of the award-winning book, *Purely Positive Training: Companion to Competition*, and co-author of the bestselling *Schutzhund Obedience: Training in Drive*. She has trained dogs for more than 30 years in a variety of disciplines.

Introduction

On a beautiful September morning, thousands of people said good-bye to their families and went to work. Others boarded transcontinental flights in Boston, Newark and Washington for business or leisure travel. Then terrorists flew those airplanes into the World Trade Center, the Pentagon and a field in Pennsylvania, as the world watched in abject horror.

But from the smoke and rubble, the world also saw a finer side of humanity as police and firefighters combed the smoldering wreckage for survivors and victims. And they watched search dog and handler teams pick their way through crumbled concrete, shattered glass and twisted steel.

Because of these devastating events and the evolving world of search dogs, we decided to update and expand this book so that we could better help people who are interested in search work, whether wilderness or disaster.

In the 1991 edition of this book, we were somewhat restricted in length, thereby limiting what we could cover in the complicated world of training search dogs. This revised, second edition has been greatly expanded. Consequently, we have been able to update training methods that were first set out in the original edition, as well as being able to add new ones.

One of the new additions to this book addresses the rise of "cadaver dog" training. Here, we set forth ARDA's view of cadaver dogs, differentiating between wilderness search dogs who should—and can—find missing people, both dead and alive, and dogs trained to find the tiniest of human remains—who we call "forensic cadaver dogs."

Another change responds to an increased interest in disaster training. This is due in large part to the development of Urban Search and Rescue Task Forces by the Federal Emergency Management Agency (FEMA). Disaster training has its own requirements for both dogs and handlers, and these are often different from what a wilderness search team requires. Because of this, we have added the latest training methods for this difficult work.

While much has changed since 1991, much has stayed the same. ARDA's standards and training methods are as valid today as they were 10 years ago. Handling a search dog remains demanding—often dangerous—work that is still one of the most rewarding "jobs" you will ever have. We sincerely hope this book helps you achieve the highest level of proficiency. Someone's life may depend on you.

Good luck, and good training.

Alice Stanley
Spotsylvania, Virginia

SEARCH and RESCUE

**AMERICAN RESCUE
DOG ASSOCIATION**

1

Forming the American Rescue Dog Association

In 1961 a little girl became lost in Snohomish, Washington. The two family dogs had gone out with her. One stayed but the other returned home. With encouragement from her family, the second dog led them back to the child. Unknown to the girl and her family, this one search would have a profound effect on the search and rescue movement throughout the United States. From this incident would flow, indirectly, the development of the air-scenting search dog, the search dog unit concept and, eventually, the American Rescue Dog Association (ARDA).

Bill and Jean Syrotuck were members of the German Shepherd Dog Club of Washington State and, while their interest at the time was obedience, the lost child and the family dog's role in finding her fascinated them. They decided it would be worthwhile to train their dogs to search for lost people. With others in the club, they formed the Search Dog Committee.

In the early 1960s tracking dogs were the standard canine tool for lost-person searches, so the Search Dog Committee members trained their dogs to track. They felt credibility could best be gained if each dog achieved an American Kennel Club (AKC) tracking title. When the training had progressed sufficiently, they scheduled a tracking test under a strict German judge. When they arrived at the test site, however, they found an unexpected obstacle: The entire field had been sprayed with a fertilizer containing cow manure. To make matters worse, the weather was warm and humid with stagnant air conditions. Even the dogs who managed to complete the test were marked "Failed" because they tracked with their noses too far from the ground.

Air Scenting

Hank Wilcox, a former military dog handler, suggested that the committee train their dogs for air scenting instead of tracking. The fiasco at the tracking test—and the realization of a tracking dog's limitations (due to contamination of the track, time and weather)—led the committee to heed Hank's suggestion. They began using the same method to locate people that Hank had used to search for downed aircraft during World War II. As Hank had trained his dogs to sniff out aircraft fuel, they would train theirs to smell airborne human scent.

TRANSITION TRAINING

The transition from tracking to air scenting was not easy. Handlers of tracking dogs weren't convinced that air scenting was a better method for dogs to find people. The properties of airborne scent were relatively unresearched, although military scout dogs had used this technique for years. To be successful, committee members who believed in air scenting began an extensive study and development program. Two things worked in their favor: German Shepherd Dogs proved to be

Bill Syrotuck. *National Park Service*

natural air scenters, and the Syrotucks were both involved in scientific research that they could apply to dog training. Bill Syrotuck's research was in applied physics, with an emphasis on statistical studies. It was this research that led to Bill's pioneering work with victim behavior and furthered his ability to determine the highest probability areas for searching. Jean Syrotuck had a degree in nursing and worked for twenty years in medical research at the University of Washington. She specialized in environmental health, nutrition and dermatology — an area which allowed her to study skin rafts for purposes of determining what human scent was to dogs. The Syrotuck's early efforts created the air-scenting search dog techniques that are used throughout our country today.

Early on, the Syrotucks discovered that dogs who were originally trained to track tended to remain "ground oriented,"—thereby potentially missing an airborne scent. But dogs who learned to air scent first remained with that scent unless they encountered a very recent "hot" track.

After several years of training—which included giving demonstrations to the local sheriff's department—the Search Dog Committee responded to its first search in July 1965. The committee was asked to search the site of a train wreck. Although all railroad personnel had been accounted for, workers reported a strong odor, and the authorities wanted to make sure a hitchhiker had not been aboard the train and was now buried in the wreckage. The dogs performed admirably. Luckily, they found no one buried in the wreckage. The strong odor was suspected to be grain fermenting in one of the cars.

NEW ORGANIZATIONS EMERGE

In 1969, the Search Dog Committee decided to separate from the German Shepherd Dog Club of Washington State. Two organizations were formed from their original Search Dog Committee: the German Shepherd Search and Rescue Dog Association (SARDA) and the German Shepherd Search Dogs of Washington State. The Syrotucks founded and led SARDA, from which evolved the first national search dog organization bonded by the same training methods, standards and tests: the American Rescue Dog Association (ARDA). More training, research

and refinement followed, as SARDA gradually developed standards and tests for dogs and handlers. When the early evaluation tests were questioned because the weather had changed between the time a "victim" was placed and the team being tested entered the field, experienced dogs would work the test to see if the problem was with the test or with the new dog/handler team. The more experienced teams would solve the problem easily, thereby showing the validity of the test. Each dog was required to pass five separate tests (a trail or "hasty search," open field, light brush, dense brush and a multiple-victim problem lasting several hours). After SARDA had refined these tests and put them in

Jean Syrotuck Whittle. *Bill Syrotuck*

written form, they were adopted in 1972 as the basis for ARDA's standards. Today, they remain an accurate indication of a team's proficiency.

New Concepts: What the Dogs Taught Us

Since air-scenting search work was a totally new concept, many training methods were tried, discarded and replaced. Among the most critical of these was motivation. Handlers found that praise alone was an insufficient reward. They needed a stronger reward. And, as is often the case, a dog solved this dilemma.

THE IMPORTANCE OF STICK PLAY

Bill Syrotuck's German Sheperd Dog, Randy, was an avid retriever who loved to play with a stick. After finding a victim, Randy was often rewarded with a game of fetch. On one training problem, Randy found his victim while out of Bill's sight. In his enthusiasm, Randy picked up a stick and carried it back to Bill. Bill suddenly realized two things: Play reward could serve as a training technique, and a dog could return to his handler after he made a find. Not only did Randy show the way to the ideal reward system, but he also helped create what today is known as the *recall/refind*, where the dogs return to their handlers (recall) and then lead them back to the victim (refind). The refind proved invaluable on actual missions where victims were unconscious, hidden in dense underbrush, or under cover of darkness, when a handler's vision was greatly reduced. While the Syrotucks thought play *might* be an excellent reward, their remaining doubts were dispelled with a visit to Texas' Lackland Air Force Base in 1971. At Lackland, the Syrotucks saw the success Air Force handlers had in training drug dogs by using tug-of-war—or other games—as a reward. From this time on, play became the standard reward in the Seattle unit and, eventually, throughout ARDA. Not only did dogs respond eagerly to play, but handlers were forced to spend more time praising dogs when they repeatedly returned with a ball or a stick (sticks were preferred, since one was always available in the woods). Older dogs who showed no interest in play underwent extensive "play-training" sessions at home. Stick play had the added benefit of increasing an indifferent dog's willingness to approach a stranger, for the dog soon learned that strangers could be coaxed into exciting play sessions. This bond enabled dogs to look eagerly for people whom they did not know. This training method is still valid some 30 years later.

THE TEAM: DOG AND HANDLER UNITS

As training for dogs and handlers was developed and refined, the concept of *search dog units* also evolved. The need for units became clear when a sheriff complained that even with two Bloodhounds at his disposal, at times neither dog was available when he was needed. From its beginning, SARDA realized multiple teams meant

SARDA found stick play to be the ideal reward system. *Tony Campion*

at least one dog was always available. As they trained these multiple teams, time dictated that several handlers had to practice simultaneously, with each working problems in different areas. This training led to the realization that the same technique could be applied on actual searches. Three or more dogs deployed simultaneously could cover large areas rapidly—this could mean the difference between finding a missing person dead or alive. A unit of multiple dog/handler teams needed a strong support organization. This organization consisted of highly trained base-camp personnel who maintained radio contact with handlers in the field, arranged for unit logistics and served as liaisons with requesting agencies. Today, all ARDA units operate the same way—by sending several dog/handler teams and base camp personnel on each search. SARDA's reputation as a professional, successful unit grew. Their help was requested in searches across the country—from Alaska to Puerto Rico. Because of the professional behavior of both dogs and handlers, the Air Force Rescue and Recovery Service at Scott Air Force Base in Illinois began flying SARDA teams on military aircraft to distant searches. The Air Force had not always experienced good results when flying dogs. There were cases of air crew members being bitten and of dogs being sick. Some crews had such negative attitudes that they would only fly dogs who were muzzled or crated. SARDA members adhered to these rules, but over time the friendly and professional conduct of the dogs led to a softening of the crews' attitudes. The much looser

SARDA responded to missions around the country, including this one at the Grand Canyon.
Bill Syrotuck

requirements seen today are a result of the exemplary behavior and training of SARDA dogs.

Forming ARDA

Word of the Seattle unit's work spread, both through missions around the country and articles in magazines such as the *German Shepherd Dog Review* (published by the German Shepherd Dog Club of America). As a result, new units were formed in New Jersey (1971), New York (1971), New Mexico (1971) and Texas (1972). Along with SARDA, these units combined to form the American Rescue Dog Association in 1972, under the guidance and tutelage of the Syrotucks. SARDA's standards became ARDA's standards. These new units became the beneficiaries of the Syrotucks' years of experimentation and experience.

NAMING ARDA

The American Rescue Dog Association name was chosen because it hinted at the organization's humanitarian purpose. Technically, the dogs "searched," while the handlers and other people performed the actual "rescue." However, the term *search dogs* had multiple meanings—from dogs who looked for explosives, to those who sought criminals. *Rescue* conjured up life-saving activities—and the American Rescue Dog Association did, in fact, perform rescues with dogs.

EVALUATION SYSTEMS

Bill, Jean and others in SARDA carefully guided the new units, demanding the same high standards as they did in their own. To ensure these standards were met, they developed membership levels and an evaluation system that each unit was required to pass before advancing to the next level.

The first full ARDA evaluation was given to both the New York and New Jersey units in September 1977. Two members from the Seattle unit spent three days testing every aspect of the applicant unit. Each dog/handler team had to pass at least one of the five field problems. These ranged from a "hasty search" along a path to a search that lasted three hours or more with multiple victims to be found. The unit's "specialists"—the operational leader, medical officer and communications officer—had to answer a battery of verbal questions, and all unit members had to pass a written test covering their overall knowledge of search and rescue. Personal and unit equipment were checked to ensure the group could handle any eventuality in the field. Handlers were picked for the physical fitness test (they had to run three miles in 30 minutes), while dogs were put through obedience, obstacle and swimming tests. The culmination of the evaluation was a mock search, where the unit was expected to perform as though on an actual mission. The operational leader conducted the necessary interviews, assessed the search problem and assigned personnel to the field. Radio communications were judged for professionalism. Base personnel were observed to see if they adequately maintained a radio log and maps showing the progress of the search, knew where the handlers were in the field, kept food and drink available and dealt appropriately with the evaluators, who role-played as members of the law enforcement agency conducting the search, the family and the media. Invariably, one of the "victims" required medical evacuation and the unit was assessed on its ability to treat and safely evacuate an "injured person."

After a unit had been awarded Provisional status—and had gained further search experience—it could request another evaluation to achieve the highest level: Full Unit. A Full Unit was given voting privileges on the ARDA Board of Directors and was also considered qualified for out-of-state missions. However, this status did not come with a lifetime guarantee. Each unit still had to pass an ARDA evaluation every three years to ensure it maintained the high proficiency level required for Full Unit status. These evaluations are severe, no-nonsense tests of a unit's capabilities.

AVALANCHE AND DISASTER WORK

While Europeans have used dogs to recover avalanche victims since the late 1930s, the United States did not use them in this capacity until the Seattle unit cross-trained their dogs for avalanche work in the late 1960s. SARDA found that it was easy for the dogs to transfer from searching for a wilderness victim to searching for an avalanche victim. A different command ("look for him/her") was used to cue the dog that the person was under the surface. The dog would then perform a much closer quartering search pattern. In 1969, a SARDA dog handled by Jean Syrotuck made the first avalanche find by an American-trained dog, on a victim buried under seven feet of snow on Mt. Rainier. In 1969, SARDA members became interested in training dogs for disaster work. Bill Syrotuck developed a friendship with Richard Radacovics of the Austrian Rescue Dog Brigade. This friendship led to an exchange of visits, with Radacovics visiting Seattle in 1971 and 1972. In 1973, Bill visited Austria, Germany, Switzerland, England and Scotland to study and discuss various aspects of avalanche and disaster techniques. Each learned from the other and, based on these discussions, SARDA devised agility and search training methods designed to prepare teams for disaster situations.

Search and Rescue Pioneers

The Syrotucks' research was not restricted to search dogs. Jean—a registered nurse—was particularly interested in wilderness medical emergencies. She wrote

In 1973, Bill Syrotuck visited Europe and the British Isles to share training techniques. *Bill Syrotuck*

about hypothermia long before it was a household word. Jean was also concerned with the nutrition needed by handlers to sustain themselves for days—often under the adverse conditions of a search. Her writing soon supplemented each ARDA unit member's formal first-aid training. This was especially critical in the 1970s, when volunteer search and rescue was in its infancy and standard first-aid courses offered little training on illnesses and injuries unique to the wilderness.

ARDA dogs were well-behaved during transport by the U.S. Air Force. *Bill Syrotuck*

LOST PERSON BEHAVIOR

While Jean pursued interests in medicine, Bill became intrigued by the behavior of lost persons. In an effort to determine if there was a pattern to their behavior that could aid search planners, Bill developed a questionnaire and began compiling statistics from around the country. This research produced the first study in the field, *Analysis of Lost Person Behavior* (Arner Publications, 1976). In addition to his studies on subject behavior, Bill also assessed search techniques used by grid (foot) searchers. The Explorer Search and Rescue Troop in Seattle was deeply committed to searching and their efforts to refine grid searching techniques aided Bill in preparing booklets on those techniques. Bill's interest in search dogs never waned, even as he researched other areas. In 1972 he published *Scent and the Scenting Dog* (Arner Publications), which still serves as the basis for understanding—as best we can—what human scent is to dogs and how that scent is transmitted. At the time Bill was working on the book, Jean worked for the Department of Environmental Health, where she had access to a vast medical library. The material in that library—combined with her training and work in the field of dermatology—led to much of the scientific explanation of skin rafts (discarded human skin cells) and their relation to the scenting dog. A combination of scientific and in-field research by both Bill and Jean was compiled in this pioneering book, which has been translated into both German and French.

THE FOUNDATION OF SEARCH AND RESCUE

The Syrotucks' early work formed the foundation of many aspects of search and rescue as we know it today. Bill's research served as the basis for much of the material contained in search management courses offered throughout the nation. The state of Washington became the center of research on techniques to improve a missing person's chance of survival. The Explorer Scouts, the state's Emergency Services directors (Hal Foss and later Rick LaValla), Bill Wade of the National

Maps and mission reports are a critical part of any search. *Penny Sullivan*

Park Service and the Syrotucks collectively helped to change search and rescue from a disorganized walk through the woods into a sophisticated, systematic approach.

By 1976, ARDA was flourishing, yet still needed Bill's sure and steady guidance. The National Association for Search and Rescue (NASAR) was a relatively new and growing umbrella organization for all search and rescue organizations (not just dog units), which relied heavily upon Bill's pioneering work. But in the fall of that year, at age 46, Bill suffered a fatal heart attack. He was posthumously awarded NASAR's highest honor, the Hal Foss Award. Upon Bill's death, Jean became president of ARDA, which continued to grow under her leadership.

Every search dog handler and every person found by search and rescue dogs owe Bill and Jean Syrotuck—and the Seattle unit—a tremendous debt of gratitude. This book is dedicated to them and the standards they developed. It is our hope that the information contained in the following chapters will help people interested in search and rescue to achieve the skills that Bill, Jean and their team members knew were necessary to save a life.

Trained search dogs from around the country in photo taken during a 1977 ARDA Board meeting.
Bob Koenig

2

Before You Begin

No one will become a skilled search dog handler by reading this book alone. At some point, you will need instruction from an experienced handler. And even when you have such help, how good you and your dog become will depend upon your dedication, the amount of time you spend and your willingness to broaden your knowledge.

You can attain adequate first-aid training by taking courses in your area. You can learn map and compass skills through orienteering clubs. And you can obedience train your dog by participating in kennel club classes.

Training Methods and Standards

There are no local courses available for search dog training, unless a search dog unit already exists in your area. If there is such a unit, attend a few training sessions and observe their methods and standards. If the unit appears competent, based on what you have read in this book, join it. If no unit exists, or if the closest unit does not meet your expectations, consider forming one of your own. Instructors are available to present weekend seminars to potential ARDA units. Contact the American Rescue Dog Association, P.O. Box 151, Chester, New York 10918. For more information, visit our Web site at www.ardainc.org.

To form a search and rescue unit, you will need at least four dog/handler teams and one base camp operator. Accomplishing all the other training (first aid, map and compass, wilderness survival, etc.) will be much easier if you have a group pulling together for the same purpose. You must be prepared to train in all kinds of weather, day or night. You will maneuver through briers, brambles—terrain

13

ATTITUDE IS EVERYTHING

Your performance—and that of your dog—will invariably reflect your attitude. If your training is half-hearted, your dog will reflect this with a lackluster attitude. She may look more like she is out for a walk in the woods than actively searching ahead of her handler. But if you really enjoy what you are doing, so will your dog. There are few sights more rewarding than that of a happy, eager search dog bounding ahead of her handler, obviously enjoying both her work and the strong rapport she has with her handler; or the experienced dog who, after eight or more hours working in adverse weather and terrain, continues to plod persistently ahead, searching the air methodically with every step. Such teams reflect the best of search work.

You should expect the entire training process to take up to one year before you begin accepting search calls. Do not rush your training—patience produces the best results.

Once your team is operational and ready for actual missions, you will learn that training is easy compared to the real thing. In an actual mission, there is pressure—lots of it. The missing person's family is counting on you; the agency is assessing you; the media is questioning you; the victim is needing you. You are involved in a life-or-death situation.

even a rabbit would avoid. You will need to attend first aid classes for several hours each week in addition to your dog-training schedule. You will work, work harder——and then work some more. You will meet "insurmountable" problems, conquer them, and then meet new ones. You will seem to take two steps forward, and then take one step back. Your dog will appear to be a "natural," and then suddenly forget everything she was taught.

You have to be persistent and overcome these problems. Search dog handlers must be persistant above all other attributes. When others are ready to quit on a search, you must carry on until all probable areas have been covered. Even your dog must be persistent and willing to work in the worst weather and terrain. "Quit" is not a word in the search dog handler's vocabulary.

Be Prepared!

Real missions do not wait for weekends. You must be prepared to respond immediately to any call. Can you leave work for two or three days at a time, perhaps several times a month? Can you afford to pay *all* your own expenses for both training and actual missions? Are you afraid to go into the woods at night by yourself? Are you afraid of snakes, ticks and other residents of the woods? If you have trained properly, these dangers should make you appropriately cautious, not terrified. There is no such thing as a "half-trained" handler. If you do not meet *all* the training requirements, you are not mission-ready. The decision is yours. If you would rather stay out late on a Saturday night than worry about getting up early for a Sunday training session, search work probably isn't for you. If, on the other hand, this is something that you have always wanted to do and you will not stop until you are good at it, you may have what it takes.

Dog and handler teams should be prepared to work in any weather. *Bill Syrotuck*

The demand for highly-skilled dog and handler teams in the United States is high. With this book, your personal dedication, and help from experienced handlers, perhaps you too can become a search dog handler.

A strategically located search dog can cover a large expanse of territory. *Penny Sullivan*

3

Selecting the Air-Scenting Search Dog

Search training begins with the selection of a special dog who possesses the appropriate mental and physical qualities for the task, and who successfully proceeds through a great deal of specialized training. This chapter focuses on scent theory and the role it plays in search and rescue.

Search Dogs Versus Tracking Dogs

Many people think tracking dogs are the traditional search and rescue workers. And it's true—they are invaluable under the right circumstances.

Certain conditions favor the tracking dog's optimum success:

- Scent articles are necessary so dogs can discriminate between the victim and other searchers.

- If weather or time has destroyed the physical or chemical evidence of a track, the dogs cannot work.

- A single dog's reaction may adversely influence the focus of an entire search.

- The area should be cleared of other individuals.

- Family members of the victim should be removed from the area (there can be similarity of scents between relatives).

- Some tracking dog handlers assume that if there are no tracks available, then there is no person in the area—and this can be an incorrect assumption.

- Some starting point—or known tracks—of the missing individual usually should be established.

If you consider the previous list and then look at the following scenario—which describes a commonly encountered situation on an actual search—it becomes obvious that the requirements for tracking dog success are often difficult to meet.

1. Some family members or friends of the victim realize that the individual is missing.

2. Friends and family make a preliminary attempt to locate the individual (which means they tramp down the area).

3. Others in the area are recruited to help search.

4. The police are finally notified.

An ARDA handler works her dog on a track. *Chuck Wooters*

With her nose held high and her tail indicating excitement, an air-scenting dog alerts on human scent. *Dick Ness*

5. A police officer visits the area, appraises the situation, and may do some preliminary searching.

6. The police officer advises his supervisor on the situation.

7. The supervisor calls in a search-and-rescue unit.

8. The unit (finally) arrives.

Under these circumstances, a great deal of time has elapsed and the area is physically and chemically contaminated, handicapping the tracking dog.

Now consider the search dog:

■ She requires no scent article.

■ She does not require tracks.

■ The area does not have to be kept completely free of other searchers; people can continue to look while the unit is en route.

■ No starting point is required.

DIAGRAM 12 - SHEDDING OF DEAD SKIN CELLS

Diagram of skin cells ("rafts"), which shed at a rate of about 40,000 per minute. *Jean Syrotuck Whittle*

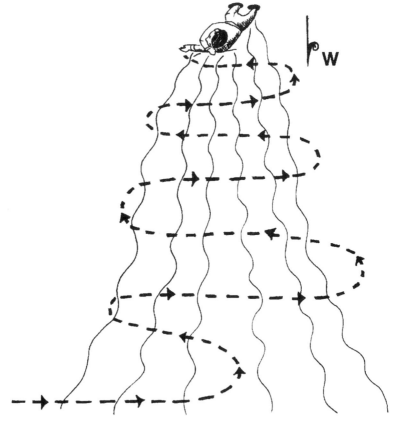

Scent is carried downwind in a cone shape, which is narrow at its source (the person) and widens with distance. Arrows indicate the path the dog follows as she works the scent cone. *Illustration by Linda Warshaw*

This dog is turning back into the scent cone. *Alice Stanley*

Dog alerting during a dense brush problem. *Emil Pelcak*

Of course, there are variations and each search is different, but almost all situations are more conducive to search dogs than to tracking dogs. A search dog can start off without a scent and search until she locates either a ground scent (track) or an air scent. The dog then uses either or both to locate the lost person (preferably, she will forsake a ground scent to check out a fresher air scent). It is also obvious that one search dog cannot do the job alone; it takes several dogs, with each one strategically located.

Air-scenting search dogs are based on the concept of military "scout" dogs, and they work in a similar manner. The air-scenting dog alerts her handler to the presence of another individual and then leads the handler to that individual.

Scent Theory

Before you can train a dog to find people, you must thoroughly understand what scent we *speculate* the dogs are responding to, and the effect that wind and terrain have on scent transport. In the 1960s, Bill and Jean Syrotuck did extensive research on airborne scent. The results were published in *Scent and the Scenting Dog* (available through NASAR or Barkleigh Productions, Inc.), and some important points from that book are covered here.

RAFTS

Humans constantly shed small, cornflake-shaped dead skin cells known as *rafts*, which are discarded at the rate of about 40,000 per minute. Each raft carries bacteria and vapor representing the unique, individual scent of the person. This is the scent sought by the trained dog. These rafts are picked up and carried by air and wind currents. They are dispersed downwind in a conelike shape that is narrow and concentrated at its source (the person), but widens as the distance grows. Trained dogs can be observed literally working the cone in open fields as they zigzag back and forth, in and out of the scent.

Different terrain and wind currents have a major impact on the dispersion of scent, and each search will present its own problems. The first day of searching may be in open woods with a nice breeze; the second day may be through dense woods in hot, windless conditions. Handlers must be well versed in the effect all these factors have on scent so that they can adapt their search plan accordingly.

TERRAIN

Terrain plays a role in determining how the dog is worked. Handlers in even the early stages of training must understand the effect that terrain has on scent behavior.

Open Fields

On days with a steady breeze, a trained dog should have no trouble picking up and following an airborne scent in an open field. An eager dog should alert and move in from a distance of 200 to 300 feet or more. This is true even if the victim has been in place only a short time (15 to 30 minutes). A lighter breeze or a very still day also produces a good alert from a distance of 100 feet or more. Strong, gusty winds create the most problems because they can rapidly disperse scent. Shifting winds make a search pattern difficult because you may originally start in a downwind direction, only to discover that the wind has shifted and you are now working upwind. In such instances, the best approach is to remain with your original pattern—the wind will continue to shift and any attempt to keep up with it will leave you wandering aimlessly around the field.

Light Brush

Light brush is defined as space that includes open or wooded areas with some brush or small woodpiles. Light brush problems should not pose any real difficulty for the dog—the brush should not be so thick that it blocks or drastically changes scent flow.

Heavy Brush

Heavy brush may be found in thick woods or unmowed fields. A heavy brush area may include brier patches and large woodpiles. Still, hot days combined with heavy brush can produce extremely difficult searching conditions because the scent will remain near the victim. Detection and ranging distances will be greatly reduced. Relatively close sweeps of perhaps 100 feet or less will be necessary for accurate coverage.

Woods

Woods can vary from an open pine forest to a swamp with large trees and very dense brush. Open woods are frequently a joy to search. Dense woods will try both your—and your dog's—patience, particularly on hot days or in the dark. Wind velocity and terrain dictate each handler's approach to this problem. Open woods in flat terrain should not be much more difficult than an open field search. Dense woods will be similar to heavy brush problems.

Drainages

Drainages or ravines can have a definite effect on scent behavior. Since hot air rises, a drainage search during the day should be conducted along the top of the hill on the downwind side. Since cool air falls, an evening search should be conducted in the drainage itself. These search patterns should cover not only the drainage, but the slopes as well.

Drainages can also funnel scent so that it flows somewhat like a stream. If alerts are recorded in a drainage but the dog is unable to work the scent out, a careful study of terrain and airflow may reveal a funneling effect. A more thorough search can then be made of upwind areas from which the scent may be emanating.

SPECIAL CONDITIONS

On occasion, handlers will encounter the following conditions during a search.

Looping

Looping is sometimes found in still wind conditions. When looping occurs, the scent is carried on an updraft above the subject, transported aloft for a few hundred feet (or farther), and then dropped back down. The dog will alert but then lose the scent because there is nothing between the subject and the point where the scent dropped. This situation makes recording alerts so important. If one or more

This eager search dog obviously enjoys her work. *Dick Ness*

Scent along a small drainage is deflected by downdrafts. *Linda Warshaw*

Looping: In still wind conditions, an updraft may carry scent aloft, transport it for some distance and then drop it back down. *Linda Warshaw*

Chimney Effect: During the day, warm air rises upslope from drainages. *Linda Warshaw*

dogs alert in an area without making a find, that area should be rechecked fairly closely. If the alert was recorded by a handler who was only halfway through a sector, however, continuing a normal search pattern often resolves the problem.

Chimney Effect and Eddying

The chimney effect is an upward air flow caused by warm air (see "Drainages"). Eddying is air that swirls along cliff walls, tree lines and similar obstructions and may disperse scent in several directions. While scent in these conditions may cause some confusion for dogs, a skilled team should have little trouble working through it. Handlers should not be so concerned with these factors that they continually alter their search plan to compensate.

Pooling

Low areas collect scent, just as they do water. As with looping, a scent pool may produce an alert that the dog cannot work to its source because of shifting winds. These alerts must be marked on both the handler's and the base maps. Handlers should assess the terrain to see what features may have funneled the scent to that particular location. When evaluating possible origination points, bear in mind that scent can be carried for long distances before it pools. Pooling is frequently seen in the cool evening hours when air flows downhill. It may well be encountered during hasty night searches of drainages or similar terrain.

Eddying: Swirling winds along tree lines, cliffs and the like may disperse scent in several directions. *Linda Warshaw*

Pooling: Low areas collect scent just as they do water. *Linda Warshaw*

ADAPTING FOR SUCCESS

Few of the conditions described will totally defeat or deter a well-trained dog and handler team. Do not use these scent behaviors as an excuse for poor performances. To be sure, wind and terrain can combine to make a dog miss her victim, but such occurrences are extremely rare. Experienced handlers learn to adapt their strategy to existing conditions, and experienced dogs learn to range persistently to find the source of a scent.

As you train your dog, you should be aware of wind velocity and direction from the very start. Also keep in mind the effect that terrain has upon these factors. Your dog's success depends upon your knowledge of how to approach each problem.

Selecting Your Search Dog

Before you choose a particular dog, you should decide which *breed* is most suitable for your purposes. When you make this decision, consider the following: short-coated dogs may have trouble working in extreme heat and cold; long-haired breeds may also have problems in extreme heat as well as being prone to briarmatted coats. Extremely short-nosed dogs usually don't have the appropriate scenting ability, and sporting breeds with inbred game instinct may be easily distracted by wildlife.

ARDA members frequently have had extensive experience with a variety of breeds, but all agree on the suitability of German Shepherd Dogs. ARDA members use German Shepherds exclusively. We require that our dogs be:

- Double-coated to provide protection and serve as natural insulation for weather extremes

- Structured efficiently, thus allowing them to gait hour after hour without tiring

- Small and agile enough to be easily transported in helicopters, etc., yet large enough to handle rough terrain

- Highly intelligent and trainable

- Equipped with proven scenting ability

- Able to strongly bond with their handlers, and have the resultant eager-to-please attitude that is critical to a successful search dog

- Lacking an inbred game instinct that would make them easily distracted by other animals

While ARDA uses German Shepherd Dogs exclusively, other breeds are also successfully used in search work. You must decide which breed suits both you and the work. Regardless of your choice, the training methods presented in this book are still appropriate.

SELECTING A PUPPY

Choosing a puppy with all the mental and physical qualities necessary to be a search and rescue dog is very important. You are not only selecting a search dog,

ARDA found that the German Shepherd Dog is ideal for search work. *Bill Syrotuck*

A strong play drive is essential for search dogs. *Roseann Keller*

but also a companion who will hopefully be with you for many years. There are a number of tests that can reveal certain qualities, but three things are most important: a friendly, inquisitive personality; a strong play drive; and a sound physical structure.

Observing the Parents

When you observe a litter of puppies, bear in mind that to a great extent, temperament is inherited. If either parent or both parents are extremely shy or overly aggressive, you should consider looking elsewhere for your dog. It's wise to observe the parents as well as the puppies so that you can make a sound assessment of temperament.

Shy Dogs. A shy dog will look and act frightened, tuck her tail, look for a place to hide or cringe behind her owner. Fear biters are pathetically terrified dogs who will, when cornered, bite their "tormentor." A puppy who flees, or whose sire and/or dam exhibit this temperament, should be immediately rejected.

Aggressive Dogs. Dogs behave aggressively because of natural instinct, training or abuse. Some breeders strive for dogs who show "pronounced courage," which is tested through Schutzhund—or protection—trials. These dogs generally have very sound temperaments; their aggressive behavior is carefully taught and controlled through obedience training. Puppies from such parents are usually willing to try new things and are undaunted by strange people, sounds and places.

Other aggressive dogs have owners who are very self-impressed when their dogs show "protection" by hitting a fence, barking and jumping. These dogs are rarely controlled or trained properly; many have simply been tormented into meanness. Puppies from these dogs are a risk.

Ideal Parents. Ideal puppy parents will appear friendly or a bit reserved (German Shepherds are expected to be friendly but reserved toward strangers), showing no signs of fear or aggression. They will act self-assured and content.

When you observe the parents, note how well they jump vertically (along a fence or up on a table). Strong jumpers indicate an agile structure, and your puppy will undergo training that requires a great deal of agility.

EVALUATING THE LITTER

Once you have seen the puppy's parents and are satisfied with their temperament, you will face one of the most challenging tasks of the aspiring search dog handler: picking the right puppy. There they are, fluffy balls of energy and innocence, their little minds totally uncluttered—just waiting to be stuffed full of all that training. How do you choose?

Before you make a decision based on what you *can* see, you need to learn about what you *cannot* see. Ask the breeder if the puppies have had their initial shots, worming and a health check by a veterinarian. Reputable breeders will request—or even require—that you have the pup checked by your own veterinarian within 48 hours of purchase. Most breeders place a guarantee on breeds that are susceptible to hip dysplasia. This guarantee often includes replacing the dog if she develops the disease within two years. Ask the breeder if one or both parents have been X-rayed for hip and elbow dysplasia and, if so, whether they are listed with PennHIP or the Orthopedic Foundation for Animals (OFA), which rates the degree of dysplasia. A puppy with parents that were both X-rayed "normal" stands a good chance of avoiding this crippling disease.

Personality

Once you determine health matters, you can begin to assess the dog's individual personality. Generally, house-raised puppies are more people-oriented than ones who have spent most of their time in a kennel. House puppies have probably had much more socialization and play. Don't forget that the early experiences and stimulation of puppies has a profound effect on their mental development.

You want a puppy who eagerly comes to greet you. A pup who stays alone in a corner is showing the first signs of shyness and should be avoided. This puppy may be the runt of the litter who has been shoved to the bottom of the pack. Some runts fight back and refuse to accept a lower station in life; these may work fine as search dogs and should not be rejected simply because they are the runt (although their smaller size at maturity may be a hindrance). A dog who cowers—whether a runt or not—will never meet your expectations.

You do not want a bully, either—the one who "leads" the pack. Unless you are an experienced dog trainer, a bully will try to test and control other dogs—and even you—at every turn. She may look cute and sassy now, but your amusement will wane when she reaches 80-plus pounds.

The best puppy is the "middle child," the one who neither dominates the litter nor hides in a corner. Once you have eliminated any bullies or runts, take the remaining pups away individually. Watch for the one who, after the initial greeting, starts to investigate her surroundings. Search dogs must be inquisitive. A puppy who curls up in your lap—while perhaps flattering—will probably be too laid back for searching. You want a puppy who shows zest and curiosity.

Play Drive

Give all remaining contenders the second important test: play drive. You will need a small ball or a rag for tug-of-war. If the puppy runs after the ball and picks it up, or gleefully grabs the rag, you have a prime candidate. If she brings the ball back to you, so much the better. If the puppy runs after the ball, picks it up and immediately drops it or simply bats at it with her paw, there is still a good chance you can bring out her latent play drive. However, you should only take this play-reluctant pup if all her other qualities are outstanding.

A puppy who shows no interest in play should be rejected. A strong play drive is critical to your final success. Without it, you may never have a dog who will continue to work hour after hour, day after day, in the worst weather and terrain.

TRAINING AN OLDER DOG

You may already have a dog or be offered an older animal for search training. Depending upon the dog's age and background, she may be entirely suitable.

As with a puppy, you want a friendly dog who is voice-responsive and exhibits a strong play drive. Many older dogs with reasonable experience among people will be outgoing enough. The major problem is usually a lack of play interest if their owners did not spend much time throwing a ball or a stick. Some of these dogs *can* be taught to play, but the amount of time spent in this effort could be better used training the dog on search problems.

When you consider an older dog, keep in mind that you will spend one year in basic training, followed by another year or two of "polishing." A three- or four-year-old dog will be five or six before she is considered experienced. Do you want to expend two or three years of effort on a dog with possibly only two to four years of field work left? You would probably be better off training a younger dog who has five to seven working years ahead of her.

Additional Puppy Tests

You should complete several other tests before making your selection. The following tests will help you find the best search dog candidate:

- Try to lead the puppy through tall grass. A pup who sits and cries lacks initiative. You want one who will happily follow you, tail held high in eagerness.

- Make a noise by hitting a pan with a spoon or a board against a fence. Do this in a nonthreatening way (the wrong application of this test could create fear where none previously existed). The mentally sound puppy may be initially startled, but will then return to investigate. When she does so, reassure her with your voice.

- Put the puppy in unusual places. Sit her on a table to see how she reacts to height; walk her across a tile or cement floor to see how she reacts to unusual footing. A puppy who cannot adjust to new experiences is not a good candidate.

- Hold the puppy on her back for a few seconds with verbal reassurance. The ideal puppy will struggle at first, then relax and submit to your control.

If two or three pups have willingly tried and passed all the tests, let your instinct make the final choice. There will be one that, for reasons you cannot explain, seems special. You can never hope to succeed in search work without a strong rapport between you and your dog. Go with that "special one."

> As far as gender is concerned, both males and females show equal ability. Choose your dog based on personality, trainability and personal preference.

Search dogs must be socialized with people of all ages. *Jane Adair*

4

Basic Training, Obedience and Agility

The first 16 weeks of a dog's life are a period of tremendous development. For the first 21 days the mental capacity of a puppy is zero. During the 21st through the 28th day, the senses (seeing, hearing, smelling, and first emotional and social stress within the litter) begin to develop. At this time, the puppy first starts to learn and should be introduced to gentle socialization.

On approximately the 28th day of life, the puppy's brain "turns on." From the 28th to the 49th day, his nervous system and brain develop to adult form. The seventh week of life is the most critical. This is the best time to wean a puppy from the litter so that he develops an attachment to his new owner. The seventh to twelfth week should introduce gentle and playful early obedience (such as kindergarten puppy training).

A dog's character is set by what he has learned up through the 16th week of life. At this time the puppy develops independence and is first introduced to discipline. Your puppy's first training starts at home. Housetraining should be his very first lesson. You should also attempt to curb chewing. With such early lessons, your puppy will learn to learn.

A young puppy has a short attention span, so you should work only 10 to 15 minutes per session, with perhaps two sessions per day. From the seventh week on you should begin socializing your puppy to interact with other dogs, other people, objects and places.

Do not use harsh corrections—they may frighten a puppy—and do not use fear as a correction. For best results, use a slow but happy pace and a vivacious-sounding voice.

Early Training

Puppies can be started on the road to search work at eight weeks of age. Their early life should consist of exposure to the outside world (called *socialization*), development of a strong play drive and the introduction to some degree of manners (called *tractability*). All must be done carefully. Mishandling of any element can quickly ruin a dog.

At this early age, the dog should encounter many varied situations while he is guided and encouraged by his owner. This experience builds the pup's confidence and the belief that his owner won't ask him to do anything harmful or impossible. He will learn that noise comes from many sources and can be both loud and soft. He will discover that moving objects have many shapes and speeds, and that people have many shapes, colors, smells and behaviors. Even a man with a cane can prove alarming to a young, inexperienced dog.

A dog who is used to trying new things with his handler will not be fazed by more new things. An outstanding demonstration of this occurred when a seasoned ARDA dog and handler were working on the edge of the cement runway at Kennedy Airport. While the dog was performing his mission, a Boeing 747 came hurtling down the runway for takeoff. The huge airplane passed the dog and handler just as its wheels left the ground. It is difficult to imagine the immensity of that aircraft and the noise of the jet engines, yet the dog—confident of his handler's judgment—did not even flinch.

SOCIALIZATION

Socialization means exposing a dog to all the sights, sounds and smells of our society in such a way that he does not feel uncomfortable. The earlier socialization begins, the better. Following are suggestions for socializing your puppy.

Handlers need to establish a close bond with their dogs. *Jane Adair*

Puppies must become comfortable in the outdoors. *Alice Stanley*

Riding in a Car

Some puppies get sick when they ride in a car. Training should start with very short (10-minute) rides two or three times a day, gradually increasing to one-hour trips.

Staying in the Car

Some puppies cry, whine and tear upholstery when they are first left alone in a car. Puppies should be left (supervised) in cars for very short periods—no more than 10 minutes at a time. As you increase the amount of time, supervision should become intermittent. Gradually increase from 10 minutes to 60; obviously, do not do this on a hot day. Use this opportunity to teach your puppy the Stay command. He will soon learn that he can't go with you when given that command. He will also become reassured when you always return. Your puppy should learn to stay in the car even if the windows or doors are left wide open.

Your puppy shouldn't bark at strangers who pass by, and he should learn to let authorized persons into the car—including gas station attendants. The reason for this training becomes obvious on a search: A barking search dog does not lend comfort to the family of a missing person. There will also be occasions when a handler will ask someone to get items from his vehicle while the dog is inside.

Unstable Footing

Some puppies go to pieces on slick floors and other unstable surfaces. Pups should be exposed to surfaces that are very smooth, rough, soft or hard. They should become familiar with wood, cement, rocks, wobbly flooring, and moving elevators. Use caution when introducing pups to unstable footing; you don't want to scare your puppy and create problems. It is not too early to use gentle commands such as Easy. If necessary, use a leash and be ready to steady the pup if he gets frightened. As with all early training, it should be a positive experience. Using praise and play always encourages puppies.

This is also a good time to introduce your puppy to the types of footing he will encounter in wilderness and disaster training. Scramble up rock piles, steep banks, piles of dead trees or log jams. You lead the way and get the pup to scramble after you. Your puppy has to learn where to place his four feet compared to your two—and this will take some doing. With experience and familiarity, your dog will show quick improvement. Eventually you should be able to throw a stick or a favorite toy into the middle of such a pile and watch him happily scramble after it. If you are using a choke collar, be sure to remove it during this type of exercise to avoid any possible entanglement.

Walking in the Woods

Puppies need to become acquainted with the different kinds of vegetation that they will plow through on search missions. Start with light groundcover at first, graduating to heavier and heavier brush as soon as your pup is game to try it. Exercise should include little jumps, deadfall scrambling and even a careful introduction to light brambles. If your puppy will play with a ball or a stick, you can use that object to encourage him to enter a small pile of brush and retrieve the item.

Search dogs must learn how to swim. *Penny Sullivan*

Swimming

Swimming not only keeps a dog physically fit, but is necessary on many search missions. Puppies can be introduced to swimming by using an inexpensive plastic children's wading pool. Begin your puppy in very shallow water. Once he is large enough to get over the pool's wall, a well-tossed ball or stick can entice him into the water.

Problem Solving 101

Predispose your pup to think for himself and take the initiative. Some examples of successful problem solving are:

Puppies need to be introduced to different terrain and conditions, including snow.
Penny Sullivan

- Learning to push open doors that are ajar.

- Running a maze that has been set up with furniture.

- Climbing in and out of cardboard boxes that have the sides cut down.

Up the Stairs

Introduce your puppy to nonslick, closed-back stairs first. After he has mastered these, try open-back stairs. Be careful, however, since your puppy won't watch his own footing. He will see through the steps, which to him look like parallel lines.

Noises

See to it that your puppy is gradually exposed to loud noises. Introduce him to vacuum cleaners, power mowers, and the rattling of pots and pans. Gradually move on to large trucks, bulldozers and car washes. Be reassuring and give your puppy a chance to approach—and explore—each noisy item.

Living, Breathing Things

Puppies should be familiarized with infants, children, adults and senior citizens. They should be aware of the shapes and smells of other animals: dogs, horses, cows, cats, birds, skunks, porcupines and snakes. For dangerous creatures—such as snakes, porcupines and skunks—your puppy should be warned, "Leave it!" Wild animals—such as bear and deer—should be identified and left alone.

Yard Behavior

Everyone wants a dog who will stay in the yard unsupervised, without tromping through the garden or digging up the petunias. Handlers can refer to several obedience books for different approaches to this. A search dog who runs loose in the neighborhood does not add credit to his unit.

Socialization should be done gradually. Do not push your pup; let him be inquisitive and learn on his own with your encouragement. If your puppy is apprehensive, take time to let him work it out. You can also introduce him briefly to particular situations and then gradually increase his exposure. Take your pup with you in the car when you visit friends' homes, the park or woods—all places where he can be petted and played with by a variety people. Take the time to introduce him to other puppies and dogs.

Fright

A puppy should never be placed in a position of being frightened. Do not be apprehensive yourself—your nervousness will be passed along to your dog. Certainly, ensure the puppy exercises some sense of caution; otherwise, he will become so desensitized that he may fall over a cliff or walk into the rotor blades of a helicopter. But if you have the attitude that unusual environments are part of your daily life, your puppy will develop this attitude as well. Careful introduction to new situations—combined with your puppy's growing trust in you—both help ensure a confident, careful adult search dog.

PLAY DRIVE

An important part of early training also begins at this time: developing a strong play drive in your dog. If you selected a puppy who loves chasing a ball or stick, or playing tug-of-war, you have achieved only the first step. Now you must emphasize his love of play by practicing short, exciting play sessions every day. Do *not* exhaust your puppy during these sessions. At his peak of interest—when he's having a great deal of fun—put the toys away and praise him. It's best to leave him wanting more.

This is also the perfect time to introduce your puppy to playing with other people, both family members and strangers. He must learn that *any* human can be conned into a fun game—this is the entire basis of your search training. Time spent now building his play drive will prove invaluable as training progresses. You can also practice commands such as Give, Take it, Pull and Out. Make sure your pup releases toys promptly when he is told to Give. If he inadvertently nips you, yelp "Owww!" (which sounds like "puppy language"). Do not give commands in a harsh voice, since you don't want to discourage his play drive.

Tractability

Tractability is a puppy's ability to try something that you ask of him without being cowed or subdued. The word *obedience* does not really apply in regard to puppies who are less than 16 weeks old. Words are used now, not commands. And these words should be associated with behaviors that happen accidentally—or with very little persuasion. A seven-week-old puppy is not too young to start learning. When he starts to lie down because he is tired, say the word "down" in a gentle but firm voice. Furthermore, anytime he lies down for *any* reason, say the word "down." Praise him moderately when he lies down, but not too much—he may get up again.

If you watch your dog closely, you will discover that he does all the things you want him to do all by himself. He sits, stands, lies down, gets things, goes away from you, comes toward you—he may even unintentionally heel on your left side. If you attach names to these acts, your puppy will soon learn what you mean. Be consistent and use those names as often as you can. You might even introduce certain arm positions at the same time you use the words. This will give your puppy his first introduction to hand signals. No is one command that is overused and should be saved for critical situations. Leave it, Don't, Hey or Stop should be substituted for No. If you don't want your puppy to chew your favorite shoe, you can say, "Leave it!"

Remember, No should be saved for urgent situations such as chasing a car or pulling a tablecloth off a laden table. "No" in a loud, sudden voice can startle a pup into brief inaction, giving you the chance to save dishes, etc., and to follow up with, "You're not supposed to do that!" and "Leave that alone!"

Some handlers use one command for life-threatening situations where, if a dog continues his actions, he may be injured or killed, and therefore must be stopped in a split second. Single-word commands such as Stop, Halt or Freeze can be used. Upon hearing that command, the dog should not move a muscle. Teaching an instantaneous drop (Down) works equally well.

By observing your puppy's actions while you play with him, you will soon discover that you can introduce him to the following words: Heel, Sit, Down, Stand, Stay, Wait, Come, Go, Take it, Fetch, Bring, Find it, Give, Out, Want to go?, among others. As your puppy grows older these words will become commands, but for now, you will find that he responds to them quickly because you have done your homework. The precision of his performance depends on you. In search work, a crooked sit is not a penalty, but your dog must sit when he is told to. It is not necessary for him to sit precisely in front of you when he is called, but he must come immediately. Obedience is measured by a dog who does what he is told without repeated commands or the necessity of yelling.

Keep several things in mind when working with puppies:

- Their attention span is very short.

- Their vision is not the same as humans nor at the same level.

- They are not physically able to perform for long periods of time or to do strenuous exercises. They should progress in stages to match their maturing bones and muscle.

Puppies should be encouraged by a happy tone of voice and made to feel that everything is fun, fun, fun—with only occasional moments of dead seriousness.

Obedience work can be terribly mismanaged, producing a dog who does not take any initiative for fear of being reprimanded. Search dogs are not machines. They do not repeat the same set of exercises for the highest score. They often use their own initiative and talent to solve problems, since they are seldom in the same situation twice—and no two missions are ever the same. Even though your dog is the "model canine in the neighborhood," it's still a good idea to take him to regular obedience classes.

Advantages of Additional Training

If you only train your dog at home, you may end up with a sporadic training schedule. Attending obedience classes puts you on a regular schedule with weekly deadlines and required practice. This will produce a successful working relationship between you and your dog.

Obedience classes expose you and your puppy to other dogs in a new environment. There is absolutely no substitute for the commotion and distraction of an obedience class. Your dog will learn to improve his attention in the midst of confusion. By aiming for top performance and precision, you will improve your teamwork with your dog.

You will find you enjoy doing a good job—and you are bound to learn some new training ideas. You will also discover a great deal about general dog behavior by watching other people handle their dogs. This will prove valuable later on when you

ARDA dogs on a group sit-stay. *Jeff Doran*

A well-trained dog will jump over anything . . . or anyone. *Bill Syrotuck*

want to teach your own dog something new. Since there are many excellent books available on obedience training, precise methods will not be presented here.

All search dogs must learn the following basic obedience skills:

- Heeling (on and off leash)

- Recall (come)

- Drop on recall (to stop a dog instantly)

- Sit-stay and down-stay

SPECIALIZED SKILLS

In addition, search dogs need specialized obedience training. ARDA standards require that dogs pass tests on the skills listed below. These tests ensure that all dogs are obedient and calm, even with the wide variety of distractions and conditions encountered on searches.

Responding to Another Handler

The dog must heel, on lead, with another unit member.

High Jump

The dog must jump into the back of a pickup truck or an equivalent, to a height of about 36 inches (this is often required for transport at search sites).

Dog Behavior

Four dogs are loaded into the back of a pickup truck and then transferred by a handler, one dog at a time—on or off lead—to the back of a second pickup truck parked about 25 feet away. After all the dogs are transferred, the handler then moves to a position about 50 feet away and—in sight of the dogs—fires a starter pistol or a pen-gun flare. The dogs must remain calm and quiet at all times.

Accepting People

While the dogs are in the truck after the previous test, three strangers come to the truck, pat and talk to each dog. The dogs should show neither aggressive nor shy behavior.

Vehicle Behavior

With the dog in the handler's vehicle, three strangers (one at a time) pass within one or two feet of the vehicle, drop an object, pick it up and move on. They will make no aggressive moves, touch the vehicle or talk to the dog. The dog must remain calm and quiet.

Retrieving in Water

The handler throws an object 40 to 60 feet out into the water. On command, the dog retrieves and presents the object to his handler. This test assesses water entry, competent swimming and retrieving.

Long Down

Four dogs on lead are put on a down in a circle 10 feet in diameter. They will stay in that location for a period of 50 minutes under the supervision of one handler, with the handlers changing every 10 minutes. The dogs may shift, sit up and lie down again, but they must remain in the same location. This exercise practices for situations when one handler watches all the unit dogs while other handlers are eating or are otherwise occupied.

Unit dogs quietly accept being loaded in one vehicle. *Emil Pelcak*

Transportation

Four dogs are loaded in the back of a truck and transported over a dirt road, with handlers present. This test simulates transport situations frequently encountered on actual missions.

Directed Search

The handler sends the dog out by voice and/or hand signal to a minimum distance of 50 feet in order to search a particular area.

The long-down exercise is required of all ARDA dogs. *Emil Pelcak*

A multiple-use obstacle with ladder, platform, ramp and "climb-through" tire. *Doug Stanley*

Confinement

The dog is put in a very confined space, such as on the floor of a car or beneath the handler's legs. The dog must show a willingness to be confined.

Dogs should learn to come down ladders slowly, rather than jumping off them. *Jeff Doran*

Control

The dog and handler walk single file in a line with other people and dogs along a narrow trail. The dog should show good behavior on a loose lead.

AGILITY OBSTACLES

Agility training serves two purposes: it gives dogs confidence in themselves and their handlers, and it teaches dogs to handle unstable or difficult footing. Agility training is normally achieved using an obstacle course, which may include various types of ramps, planks, ladders, jumps and tunnels. All ARDA dogs undergo extensive agility training. Most units have created their own courses with a wide variety of obstacles.

As you begin your agility training, remember it is unlike training for agility competition, which is based on speed. Search agility requires the dog to be controlled and balanced enough to stop in an instant. Envision a confident search dog walking a sloped, canted steel beam suspended over a burning pit, as happened at the World Trade Center, and it is easy to see why control is far more important than speed.

Handlers should demand sits and stays on stable portions of the obstacle course. *Emil Pelcak*

Narrow planks teach balance. *James Pearson*

55-Gallon Oil Drums

When the ends are removed, these drums can be used as tunnels, particularly for young dogs—the height and circumference is less intimidating than a smaller space. These also serve as an unstable surface for older dogs to jump up on or climb over.

Ramps

Ramps can be made from wooden planks that are either smooth or equipped with "cheaters" (small boards nailed crosswise to provide a grip for the dog). Cheaters should be used for young dogs, but older dogs must eventually be able to climb a ramp without them.

Jumps

These may be bar jumps (a single board or rod suspended between two posts); broad jumps, which require a

Search dogs must learn control on the agility course. *James Pearson*

Puppies should be introduced to obstacles gently, using a favorite toy as an enticement. *Bob Snyder*

A large dog obeys the command to go through a small pipe. *Alice Stanley*

Agility training prepares dogs for the difficult footing they will encounter on search missions. *Penny Sullivan*

dog to jump *across* rather than *over;* a six-foot piece of plywood that the dog must scramble up and over; or a solid "wall" jump that is adjustable in height. Be sure the jump will "give," or fall, should the dog hit it.

Metal Highway Culvert Pipes

Not only do these make excellent tunnels, but you might have to send your dog independently through one during a search (small children may hide in them).

Teeter-Totters

Walking on a teeter-totter teaches a dog how to handle extremely unstable footing. It may consist of nothing more than a wide plank nailed to a round log.

Platforms

This may be a relatively small, square board placed at a height of about 36 inches and used to train dogs to jump vertically. A platform may also be used in combination with a ramp.

Ladders

Dogs should not attempt to climb a ladder until they are confident climbing stairs. A ladder can be extremely difficult for dogs, since it is open backed *and* more vertical than most stairs. Ladders may be used in conjunction with a platform so that the dog has somewhere to go when he reaches the top of the ladder. A child's slide at a playground serves this purpose well.

PROGRESS SLOWLY

When properly done, agility training greatly increases a dog's confidence. Do not test or proof the dog on flimsy material that may give or break under his weight. Such difficult obstacles should only be attempted when the dog is thoroughly trained, and even then it should be done cautiously.

At times it will be necessary for handlers to physically assist a dog by grasping the scruff of his neck. As part of agility training, dogs should become accustomed to being pushed, pulled and lifted from various angles.

If available, a tractor with a front-end loader or similar equipment should be used to lift dogs and handlers. This training requires trust between dogs and handlers, as well as preparing them for disaster missions where they may have to be lifted onto a rubble pile.

Proper agility and obedience training pays dividends when search teams work in rugged terrain or on disaster searches. It also develops mutual respect and confidence between dog and handler.

There are many obstacles other than those just described. With a little imagination and a minimal amount of carpentry, you can create your own variations. A well-planned obstacle course trains dogs to handle diverse situations as well as providing exciting and fun challenges for dogs and handlers.

TRAINING FOR OBSTACLE WORK

Dogs who exhibit an eager-to-please attitude will show a willingness to try any obstacle their handler asks of them. Dogs who possess this attitude—along with a strong play drive—will be undaunted by any unusual footing they may find on either wilderness or disaster missions.

Play drive can be used as motivation for agility work, just as it is for search training. As the dog completes each obstacle, reward him with a favorite toy or stick. Eventually, you can withhold play until the dog has completed the entire course. Using this method, handlers often find dogs will complete an entire course—off leash—with enthusiasm. One of the easiest ways to build fun and excitement is to work in a group with other dogs, especially those experienced and confident with various obstacles.

Safety is imperative. You must always work with one or more assistants if the obstacles are very high or potentially dangerous. *Always ensure success*. If a dog is having trouble, suspend training on that particular obstacle for a day or two and then try it again. End each session with several obstacles that the dog loves to work and on which he excels.

While working obstacles, dogs should learn a variety of commands. When asked to climb something, they should be told to Go on up or Hup! When entering a tunnel, Go on through can be used. Use words or phrases that make sense to *you* so that you can be consistent with their use. To prevent your dog from becoming too fast or simply performing the course by rote, alternate your approach to each obstacle or occasionally require your dog to come back over or through an obstacle that he has just completed.

Once your dog feels comfortable and confident on the various obstacles, you can caution him to move more slowly by using the Easy command in a low, drawn-out tone. Handlers should also start demanding Sits, Downs and Waits on the stable sections of the course. A careful Turn Around command and directed rights, lefts, ups and downs to various prominent obstacles and levels from some distance are also useful.

Puppies should be started on a small, nonthreatening course. A wide board with each end resting on a cinderblock laid on its side makes an excellent beginner's plank. Jumps should be only inches off the ground to avoid undue stress on still-developing bones and muscles. A very easygoing, gentle approach—combined with play rewards—produces a puppy who will look forward to this new game.

An eager search dog bounds ahead as her handler provides strong verbal encouragement.
Bill Syrotuck

5

Beginning
Search Training

As you begin search and rescue training you will want to keep track of your progress. What next? Are you going too fast? Without some yardstick, it is difficult to tell. We have organized the training into steps to make it easier. Your progress will depend upon your ability and knowledge, your dog's ability and knowledge and the time you are willing to invest. Training five times a week for three weeks amounts to 15 sessions. If you train only once a week, it will take more than three months to cover the same ground. It may take even longer, as your dog will tend to forget some of her training from one week to the next.

Do not start search training until you have had the dog or puppy for at least one week and have spent that week playing with her and firmly establishing that you are her master and friend. A dog's initiative to find you will depend upon her attachment to you—and this is where it all begins. For purposes of brevity, we will assume you are starting with a puppy.

Great Expectations

The ultimate success you have with your dog will depend upon establishing a firm foundation and ensuring that your dog understands what is expected of her. One of the most common mistakes made by inexperienced handlers is the assumption that, because their dog found them so readily, she must be capable of finding others with the same enthusiasm. In fact, a puppy will almost always eagerly find her handler if you've built a strong bond. Transferring this behavior to someone else is an entirely different matter. Although initially your puppy may seem successful at finding another person, this success will soon crumble if you have not built a firm foundation.

While the steps in this chapter will provide that foundation, the way you approach them ultimately will determine your success. Spending a great deal of time building your dog's play drive before you begin search training will advance your dog through the steps faster than if you train for searching and drive at the same time. If your dog has a strong "hunt" drive—exhibited by a willingness to search for a toy regardless of how long it takes her or where you have thrown it—she will progress more rapidly. A trained dog with a solid hunt drive will search for a stranger with tenacity. But take your time. Do not rush through the steps. Spending three months searching solely for the handler or taking a full year to complete all the steps is not too long. As you start training, you should use a particular collar or leash so the puppy becomes "cued" as soon as she sees that equipment.

Step 1: The Runaway Game

This is the initial introduction to both the game of "find" and the Find command. It must be fun for the puppy at all times.

> **Note:** Step 1 is for very young puppies only; older dogs should start with Step 2. If you absolutely cannot outrun the puppy—or you have an assistant readily available—going to Step 2 is perfectly acceptable.

Choose open areas that are relatively flat with small clumps of cover—grass, shrubs or weeds. Select a time of day that is not too hot or too cold. Check that there is a light breeze blowing and know the direction of the wind.

Since the puppy is very small (eight to ten weeks of age), you can generally outrun her. This exercise can be done without the aid of an assistant.

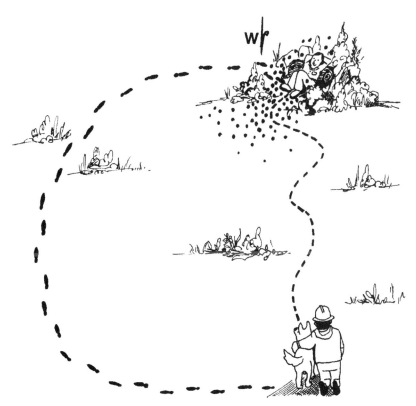

Beginning search problem: "Footprints" show the route taken by the "victim." The dotted line is the route normally taken by the dog. *Linda Warshaw*

RULES OF THE GAME

Play this game following these rules:

1. When you arrive at the area, allow your puppy a few minutes to acquaint herself with the grass, smells, noises, etc.

2. Start walking slowly with your puppy to establish her attention and get her moving along in your direction.

3. When you have her complete attention, quickly run ahead of her into the wind and call, "Here girl! Puppy! Puppy! Puppy!" Your voice and manner should sound exciting.

4. When you have outdistanced your puppy by 50 to 100 feet, flop down behind a clump of grass (out of her sight) and wait for her arrival.

If your pup does not come straight to you, give her a few moments to see if she can discover you with her nose.

If she looks stumped, make a sound or motion to attract her.

5. When the pup discovers you, lavish her with praise and a play session. Even very young puppies will grab a squeaky toy, and such interest should be encouraged from the very beginning.

Avoid startling the pup when she finds you. Many puppies temporarily freeze when they see their master in an unusual position and location (lying down in the grass). Speaking to them is usually all that is necessary to reassure them.

6. Immediately repeat the runaway game two more times.

KEEP IN MIND

Remember that a puppy is like a baby. Once you disappear, she thinks you really are gone, and won't be able to remember exactly where you went. If you planned the wind properly, your puppy will soon find you by using her nose. Dogs see motion much better than detail. If you remain frozen, your puppy won't notice you even if part of you is exposed.

When you use the same area over and over again for exercises, your puppy will associate the area with the game and become cued upon arrival.

VARIATIONS

Try the following variations:

1. Run in a small arc so that your puppy tries to shortcut the last part and starts to rely on her nose and on the airborne scent.

2. Change areas occasionally. As your puppy gets better, include areas with small ground cover.

SCHEDULE

Follow this schedule:

- Two to three times each outing.

- Several outings in close succession (not more than 10 times total).

Tim Sullivan

Runaway training: First, the handler entices the pup with a stick, then runs in a semicircle while an assistant excites the dog. *Tim Sullivan*

Next, the pup is released and races to the owner, while the assistant follows behind and provides verbal encouragement. *Tim Sullivan*

Tim Sullivan

Tim Sullivan

Finally, the owner rewards her puppy with a play session. *Tim Sullivan*

Older dogs should be started with runaway problems. *Doug Teeft*

WHEN TO GO TO NEXT STEP
Move on to Step 2 as soon as possible.

Step 2: Training with Visual Cues

This is also frequently referred to as "runaway training." Use an assistant who thoroughly understands what you are going to do. A family member is best, but sometimes a puppy is too content to stay with them instead of running after you. If Step 1 has become a great game, leaving your puppy with an assistant so that both of them can come after you, shouldn't be a problem.

Go to your usual working field. Have an assistant hold your puppy by placing one arm around her body and the other arm hooked through her collar. If you are using a choke collar, do not hold the ring—this will tighten the collar into a correctional hold. You want to contain your puppy, not correct her.

SHOW YOUR ENTHUSIASM
Talk to your puppy in an enticing and exciting voice. Augment this by clapping your hands or showing your puppy her favorite toy. While still talking and calling to your puppy, run away in a semicircular path and drop behind a bush or a clump of grass about 100 feet away. Make sure the wind is blowing your scent toward the puppy.

As you leave, your assistant should help increase the pup's curiosity by saying, "Watch him! Where's he going? Look at that!" (Your assistant should not say "Find him!" until the moment she releases the puppy. You should pause briefly between the words of encouragement and the Find command to ensure the pup distinctly hears the command.) While restraining your puppy, it's important that the assistant permit enough freedom of movement to allow the pup to squirm around in eagerness. As you disappear (by diving behind a bush), your assistant must make sure the puppy sees where you have gone, and should immediately release the puppy while urging her to "Find him! Atta girl! Find him!"

If the pup stops in confusion, your assistant also stops and should allow the puppy a chance to find your scent on her own. If this is unsuccessful, you should call out. Repeat if necessary until your puppy alerts and starts to home in on you. Then stop calling.

Lavish your puppy with praise and/or play from both you and your assistant as soon as she makes the find. Do not stand around talking about any problems. Your puppy must be rewarded immediately.

Repeat right away, two or more times, making sure that the exercise is into the wind.

REMINDERS

Here are some things to remember while working on Step 2:

- Your dog can be taken to an area on lead, but never on a Heel command. This would constitute a form of constraint when the goal of beginning a search is maximum freedom, motivation and speed.

- Never tell your dog to Stay with an assistant. You *want* her to fuss to be released. Stay is used when you want your dog to be quiet and controlled.

- Never use Come as an enticement. This is a command you want to reinforce by having your puppy come immediately and, obviously, an assistant will not let that happen. Older dogs may take a nip at any person who doesn't let them go once they hear the Come command.

SETTING UP THE PROBLEM

You should set up the problem so that your puppy leaps forward toward the point where she last saw you. This shortcuts the ground trail and encourages the dog to use air scent alone to complete the problem. If the dog finds the trail and elects to follow it at some point, allow her to do so. Try to set the next exercise with a wider semicircle so as to avoid trailing.

Don't forget:

- Use words of encouragement when your pup's head is held high and she is using the air currents.

- When a dog trails or tracks at this stage, *never* correct or reprimand her. You have asked her to find you by using her nose and you must allow her to do this the best way she knows how. It is up to you to set the problem up in such a way that air scenting is the quickest and easiest way for the pup to solve it.

- The pup *must always* succeed and make the find.

- Both you and the assistant must reflect great excitement and enthusiasm in your voices. One of the most difficult things for new handlers to learn is proper voice inflection. There is no room for shyness when you are trying to stimulate your dog's eagerness.

VARIATIONS

As soon as the pup responds well by running out eagerly, try these variations:

1. Start to call less and less while you run away. Tantalize your puppy as you leave, but not after.

2. Introduce a tug-of-war rag, a stick or a ball to bait the pup as you leave. Praise her and play with the object when the "victim" is found.

3. Increase and vary the distance from 100 to 500 feet. Vary the number of problems per outing from one to three.

4. Once the dog has a good understanding of the game and has a reliable, eager response, try a check mark problem. While the runaways have been primarily line-of-sight, this will be the first problem where the puppy must use her nose to find you. To accomplish this, you should hide in such a way that the puppy will cross and hit your scent before she gets to where she last saw you.

   To do the check mark, run across the wind until you are about 100 feet away from the puppy, then stop, turn and face her. At this point, your assistant will turn the puppy so she cannot see you. After your pup is turned, walk about halfway back toward her, but off to the side of the path you ran, angling into the wind (see the diagram on page 63). Your puppy should hit your scent before she gets to where she last saw you, so be sure the wind is blowing from behind you, across the puppy's path, as you drop down in the grass or behind a bush. As soon as you are down, your assistant will turn the pup back in your direction and release her on the Find command. The puppy should race toward where she last saw you, but hit your scent well before she gets to that point. Her nose should hook toward you as she hits the scent.

SCHEDULE

Follow this schedule:

- One to three times each outing.
- Three to five times a week.

WHEN TO GO TO NEXT STEP

The puppy is ready for Step 3 when she whines and squeaks in anticipation, and races out after release with no hesitation or uncertainty. In a breeze of five to ten miles an hour, she should be able to home in on you in an almost straight line.

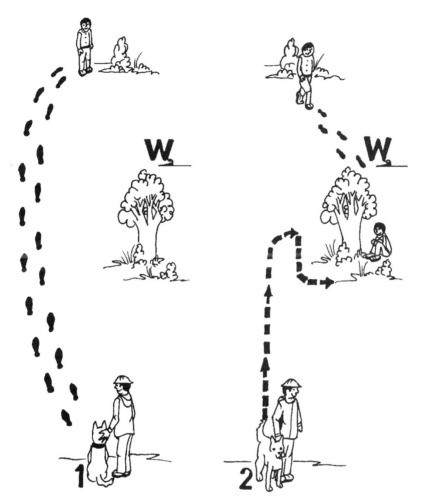

Check mark problem: After the handler runs in a semicircle, 1) an assistant turns the dog while the handler moves back into the wind and hides; 2) the dog is then turned around and released on the Find command. *Linda Warshaw*

Step 3: Increasing Time and Difficulty

This is the step that introduces other people and increases the working time and difficulty. You are preparing for Step 4, when the dog will learn to look for a "victim" *without* seeing that person leave.

The first stranger the pup finds should be a good acquaintance of the dog or a member of the family. Ideally, he should be someone with natural exuberance who likes and enjoys animals. This person should be willing to spend time playing

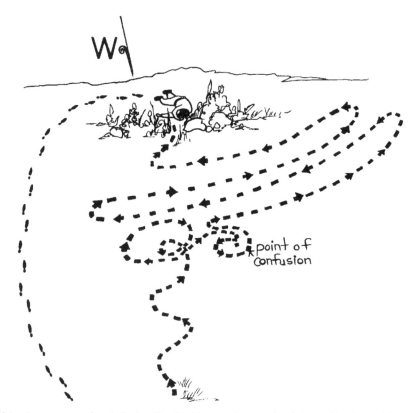

If the dog seems confused, the handler should move closer to the victim and begin semicircular sweeps until the dog hits the scent. *Linda Warshaw*

games of tug-of-war or chase the stick with the pup. He should not be shy about sounding excited while playing these games. This game-playing reward cannot be overemphasized. Initially, lavish praise and rolling and tumbling are adequate rewards. Eventually, though, this can become a "so what" situation unless the pup finds that strangers can be finagled into doing all kinds of fun things. This will be an important part of your dog's attitude toward strangers.

During Step 3, you will alternately use a friendly acquaintance and yourself as victims. Use other people for search problems as long as the dog performs well. Insert yourself as the victim each time you try something different or difficult.

Use yourself as the victim to try the following:

- Change to slightly denser brush.

- Make the pup wait three to five minutes before starting after you. Try leaving her inside the car (with supervision from the outside) where she can watch you leave, after you have said a very intriguing good-bye. You should still make a running departure because it is the best attention-getting device. You can slow down to a brisk stride for some of the easier problems done in open terrain. Be sure the dog notices you near your end point, or she may try to trail; if necessary, call out to her.

- Work these exercises at different times of day.

- Try some tall brush with a good wind sweep—a solid breeze that is fairly strong and steady, and doesn't shift—through it, but without much dead-fall. Have the assistant alert the dog with a Listen command. Be sure the victim (you) steps on lots of twigs or makes enough noise for the dog to cue on. Again, use the basic semicircle pattern into the wind.

- Begin introducing more difficult and varied terrain.

Use friends or family as victims in these exercises:

- Start with a short, easy field problem with the victim first enticing the pup and then running away, as at the beginning of Step 2. Cue the dog with, "Watch Jim! Where's Jim going?" Upon release, say, "Find him! Find Jim!" Dogs can and should learn the names of family, friends and other handlers—this is a good way to start.

- As the dog responds and performs well, increase the distance and working time, as in Step 2.

- Have the victim bait the dog with a stick or tug-of-war rag as soon as the pup will respond to this game. Always use it as a reward. Discover and use whatever is a turn-on for the dog.

- If the puppy is responding very well, use your dog's favorite friendly victim and try a light brush problem.

REMINDERS

If possible, use the same acquaintance until your dog has progressed noticeably and responds with maximum eagerness. Then you can then try one other person and alternate between the two, identifying each by name to the dog.

If at any point the dog is unable to close in (eagerly approach) on her victim, work her in a semicircle around the downwind perimeter until she reacts to the scent. Immediately reinforce the response with, "Atta girl! That's it! Find him! There he is!" *The dog must always succeed*, even if you have to walk her over to the victim (never do so in a straight-line pattern).

SCHEDULE

Follow this schedule:

- Two to three times in each session.
- Three to five times a week is most preferred.

WHEN TO GO TO NEXT STEP

The dog is ready for Step 4 when she eagerly searches for you in a variety of terrain at various times of day, with a strong close-in and an enthusiastic play session.

> *A mature dog with a strong play drive and very good handler rapport should progress rapidly through the first three steps.*

Step 4: Transferring to Nonvisual Cues

This is the lead-in to basic search work. Once you and the dog have mastered Step 4, the possibilities are unlimited. There are six exercises in this step.

EXERCISE 1

Go to the usual working field with your assistant. Have the assistant let you out of the car at Point A and then drive the dog to Point B. Your assistant will then remove the dog from the car, being careful not to reprimand her for eagerness or exuberance, yet still keeping good control. If the dog gets loose at this point, the owner should hide immediately and let the dog complete the problem.

Both dog and assistant should move to a location where they can watch the owner walk away from Point A to Point C and disappear. The assistant alerts the dog with, "Watch him! Where's he going?" The owner may have to wave his arms or call out briefly to attract the dog's attention.

The assistant releases the dog with, "Find him!" and helps get the dog into a good downwind position if the dog has any difficulty. As a last resort, you can call out once or clap your hands. Even if the dog requires some assistance from the "victim," let her complete the problem without further assistance when possible. Encourage the dog, but avoid a constant stream of chatter. Remember to reward her generously; do not shortchange praise and play while you and your assistant discuss the performance.

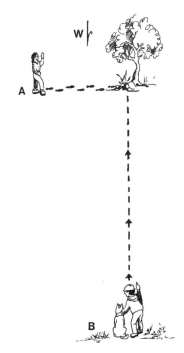

Point A to B problem: The "victim" is dropped off at Point A and the dog is taken to Point B. The dog watches the person walk across and hide, as the handler provides verbal excitement. The dog is then released on the Find command. *Linda Warshaw*

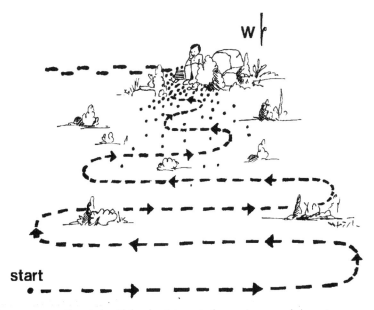

Grid an area across the wind until the dog intersects the scent cone and closes in. *Linda Warshaw*

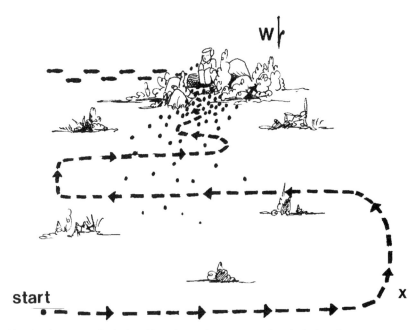

Use the shortcut method of gridding if your dog seems confused. The handler recognizes at Point X that his dog is not working properly and moves closer to the "victim" to begin sweeps. *Linda Warshaw*

EXERCISE 2

If the first exercise worked well, repeat it again in the same locale. Do not let the dog see you hide this time. The sound cue is optional.

EXERCISE 3

Repeat a third time, using no sound cues if possible. If you have any problem in the previous exercises, continue to use the sound cues for one or two days, until the dog has it mastered, then move on to the next exercise.

EXERCISE 4

Use your friend (assistant) as the victim and repeat the first three exercises in your next working session. Again, strive for minimal to no cues, except to let the dog know that you have let someone out of the car to go hide.

EXERCISE 5

Place the friend (victim) in the usual search area without the dog's knowledge. About 15 minutes later, go to the area and work the problem. The object is to keep working the dog back and forth across the wind (eventually through the scent cone) until she notices and alerts. Keep the first problem relatively short—

SCENT ARTICLES

Great items for scent work include unlaundered articles worn next to the skin (these can be T-shirts, socks, pillowcases—even a clean rag that's been worn under a shirt for several hours), and well-worn items— such as stocking hats, gloves or tennis shoes.—that aren't washed often.

Less desirable items that are awkward to carry include jackets, coats and trousers.

If an article is accidentally handled for a few moments by other people, it should not be affected. But if there is any doubt as to the validity of an article (if it *might* belong to someone else), *do not use it.*

perhaps five or ten minutes in good wind conditions. Do not let the dog lead you aimlessly through the area; decide upon your search pattern, based on wind direction, and stick with it. Break your pattern only when you know the dog has picked up and is working the victim's scent (you must know exactly where the victim is at this stage of training). Be encouraging and watch the dog like a hawk. The moment she shows an alert, encourage her with, "That's it!" When she starts to move along the scent cone toward the victim, continue to encourage her with, "Atta girl! That's it! Find him!"

If the dog appears uncertain, cut the problem short by moving in closer to the source of the scent so that the dog can pick up on it during the first or second pass.

EXERCISE 6

Introduce the dog to the use of the scent article. Use a tennis shoe, sock or T-shirt of the victim.

As you give the command, "Find Jim!" offer the scent article about one inch from the dog's nose. If the dog wishes, let her mouth or sniff the article for up to five seconds, saying, "That's Jim, let's find Jim!" If the dog is not particularly interested, *do not* force the article on her. If the article is in a bag, do not force the dog's head in the bag!

Any time the dog returns to you during the exercise, offer the scent article for a quick whiff. Again, do not insist or force her. Often a dog will recognize "Jim's" scent when you first offer the article and will need little reinforcement. Eventually, the dog will realize this scent belongs to the person she should be looking for.

REMINDERS

Never move in a straight line toward the victim. If at any time your dog seems bored or the problems are not working well, drop back to an earlier stage—with variations—when the dog was performing successfully.

Dog being given a scent article. *Penny Sullivan*

VARIATIONS

Try these variations:

1. Do longer problems in open terrain. Increase the total distance as well as the number of passes.

2. Try light brush problems with a good breeze blowing. Use other members of the family as the "victim." Use the scent article on alternate problems.

3. If your dog lacks eagerness or displays uncertainty on the close-in, spend more time on motivation by letting the dog play with the victim—or use a family member as the victim.

SCHEDULE

Follow this schedule:

- Three short problems each session.
- Three times a week.

- Practice short problems until the dog is reliably and eagerly finding the assistant, with a strong alert, close-in and play session.

- Progress to three medium to long problems (15 to 30 minutes) per session, three times a week.

WHEN TO GO TO NEXT STEP

The dog is ready for Step 5 (see Chapter 6) when:

- She understands that when you get to the area and give the Find command, a victim is there even though she has not seen or heard the victim being placed.

- She keeps searching and moving ahead of you for the full 30 minutes.

- She closes in on the victim from a distance of 90 to 150 feet in a good breeze.

- Her close-in is both certain and eager at least 90 percent of the time.

The polished dog works independently through rough terrain. *Bill Squire*

6

Advanced Search
Training

This chapter contains training methods that are intended to increase the working scope of your dog. The basic search problems presented in Steps 1 through 4 in Chapter 5 are continued here, with increasing variations.

Step 5: Improving Search Skills

Practice the following variations to enhance your dog's search skills:

1. Increase and vary the dog's working time from 30 minutes to two hours; occasionally insert 10-minute problems to keep the dog's motivation high.

2. Increase the working area up to half a square mile, or a narrower area approximately one mile long with the victim at the far end.

3. Vary the terrain. Use a mixture of light to medium to heavy brush. Start the heavy brush as somewhat shorter problems with maximum motivation.

4. Start working short, easy problems in "contaminated" areas where you know other animals and people have recently been. Try a second problem in the same areas a short time later. Be prepared to watch the dog and learn something yourself. Be prepared to assist the dog slightly.

5. Start occasionally using a complete stranger for short problems. Use a scent article.

6. Do several problems where the victim's exact location is unknown to you.

7. Start occasionally using two victims. Begin with short problems—approximately 10 minutes to find victim A, stop and praise, then move on to find victim B. Gradually increase the time to approximately 30 minutes each.

ADJUSTING YOUR DOG'S WORKING PACE

At this point in training, it is often obvious if you have a dog who works either too fast or too slow. This varies according to your dog's personality and is somewhat affected by your basic training technique. At any rate, you will probably want to speed up your dog or slow him down.

Slowing Down

With a dog who is voice-conscious (yours should be), often all you have to do is give the command, "Dusty, wait." Calling a dog's name should make him start back to you. As soon as the dog is where you want him, send him again with, "Okay, Dusty, let's find Joe!"

Practice the Wait command when you are out walking the dog, especially along trails or during obstacle course work.

If you have an especially exuberant dog who is frequently out of sight in brush, call, "Dusty, wait!" and then duck into the nearest good hiding place. Be prepared to wait for your dog to discover that you are missing and come back to find you. When he does, say "Good dog! Let's go find!" and start searching again. Repeat this several times, about 10 minutes apart, and your dog will soon start looking over his shoulder to make sure you are still there. If your dog ranges too far, his sense of responsibility should bring him back periodically to check on you. This technique produces a working pattern with the dog ranging out in large circles that loop back to his handler.

Speeding Up

Some slow dogs spend too much time sniffing out the whole environment. While this is interesting, it is not why you are out there. Allow your dog to check out the basic smell of the area for a few minutes before you start working. When he sniffs out clumps of grass, cow pies or the area around trees, he is just plain "dinking around." You don't want to turn him off to all scents in the area, because he may ignore a dropped glove. Allow him one quick sniff followed by, "Okay, let's go!" or "Leave it, let's find Linda!" If your dog is behind you, say, "Come on, let's go find her!" You should move out at a brisk pace. If you leave the dog behind, call out, "Dusty, get up here—let's go!" As soon as Dusty moves ahead of you, praise him with, "Atta boy! Let's go find Linda!"

Young dogs—and sometimes older ones—can be "turned on" by observing other eager workers do a short problem while they wait and watch from a distance.

The slow dog may need to drop back to some easier problems and work more on game playing. Dinking around generally indicates a lack of enthusiasm for the task at hand—this in turn can indicate a lack of sufficient motivation.

You may have a dog who works perfectly well in front of you (he is eager and trying), but does not get quite as far out as you would like. To increase his ranging, face one direction and start off eagerly, telling the dog, "Barry, let's find John!" As Barry races out ahead of you, move only a short distance, then veer back in the opposite direction. As the dog comes racing back toward you, send him off again with, "Atta boy! Find John!" Again, as your dog speeds out, go only a short way and then veer back to your original direction of travel.

If you use an arm signal when you send a dog out, you will soon develop a method of *directed sending*. This proves handy when you want to send your dog to check out a particular area. Directed sending is similar to a technique known as directed retrieving, which is used for bird dogs. With directed sending, you run the risk of having a dog who listens so hard for the change of direction that he doesn't pay attention with her nose. To avoid this, use these commands only informally and occasionally.

Sometimes a slow dog is the product of a slow, unenthusiastic handler. Learn to use an eager tone of voice and a brisk pace to set the working tone at the start. Do not slow your pace to stay behind the dog; if he moves slowly and you speed up, he will quicken his pace. A dog who moves out at a good clip is less likely to dink around. Learn to use your tone of voice to good advantage. *Do not* say, "Come on, let's go find him!" To the well-trained dog, "come" means "return to me"; thus you are giving conflicting commands.

Sometimes a dog is a little slow because he has been given too much play time. He may be using up all his spare energy and interest before working the problem. Play should come *after* the work session.

REMINDERS

If a dog really messes up, analyze the situation. This is how a handler learns. The odds are that you made a judgment error (the victim was not where you thought he would be or the wind was not as strong as you suspected). If you appraise the situation properly, you may recall that your dog indicated "something," but you failed to recognize it or did not follow up.

Never reprimand or punish the dog, no matter how badly he may have worked. Punishment quickly makes a dog look busy just for the sake of looking busy. There he is, sniffing up a storm and not even trying to find the victim. You will never know the difference until it is too late. Remember you can *train* a dog to use his nose, but you cannot *force* him; a dog must enjoy his job if he is eventually to work long hours in adverse conditions. If a dog is reprimanded while performing correctly and the handler is in error, the dog will become confused. Unjust reprimands may undo several months of training and impair a dog's confidence.

An advanced dog should range ahead of his handler, seeking the airborne human scent. *Jean Syrotuck Whittle*

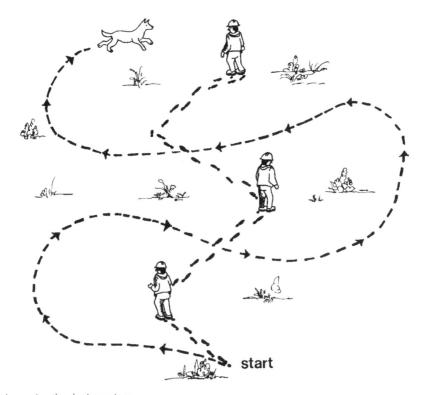

Improving the dog's ranging:
Step 1: As the dog races out ahead, the handler should veer back in the opposite direction.
Linda Warshaw

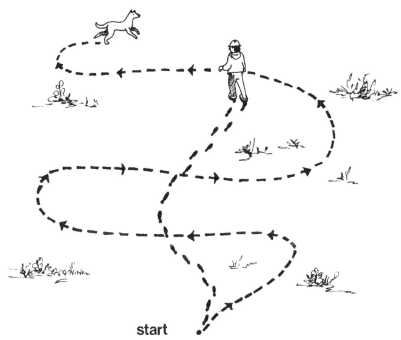

Step 2: As the dog's ranging improves, the handler reduces his zigzag pattern while still providing verbal encouragement. *Linda Warshaw*

start

Dogs, like people, are fallible. If it is a bad day for either one of you, keep the exercise short and end on a successful note.

SCHEDULE

Follow this schedule for Step 5:

- Two to three times each session
- Two to three times a week

WHEN TO GO TO NEXT STEP

The dog is ready to move on to Step 6 when:

- He alerts consistently and his alerts are easily recognized.
- He has flawless close-ins.

A dog eagerly leads his handler back to the victim on the refind. *Ray W. Jones*

- He generally works the correct distance (depending on terrain and wind conditions) from you.

Step 6: Finding an Unconscious Victim

This step concentrates on teaching your dog to find an unconscious or unresponsive person. To do this, the dog must have a foolproof method of letting you know someone is there, even if you have not noticed his alert. There are many different indications that handlers can teach their dogs to ensure they recognize the recall/refind. Some handlers train their dogs to bark at the handler, some to jump up on them and some to tug at their favorite toy. Other dogs perform the classic refind of running back to the handler and immediately returning to the find. Regardless of which method you prefer, it must be something you immediately recognize.

1. Start with a large field problem with favorable wind conditions, so that the dog picks up the scent from 100 feet or more.

2. Allow the dog to race all the way to the victim's location (he should be doing this naturally now). As he does so, move off diagonally from the victim's location.

3. When the dog reaches the victim, the victim should remain in place and respond with a quiet, engaging, "You found me. Good boy." The victim should also give the dog a friendly pat. The victim should show the ball or stick to the dog, but shouldn't let him have the object.

4. Allow the dog time to greet the victim and nose around him, then call the dog back. As the dog returns to you, say, "Good boy! Did you find him? Where is he? *Show* me!" The dog may start back immediately and should be encouraged.

   If the dog is uncertain, start off toward the victim's location with the Find command. As soon as the dog heads toward the victim, praise and encourage him forward. Hurry after him to reinforce him the whole way.

5. Praise and play immediately after the dog leads you to the victim.

Practice this regularly, but on some occasions it should be omitted—particularly when the dog alerts from a short distance. The dog may think you are not too bright, standing a few feet away while the victim is obviously right there. He may not understand what you are trying to do.

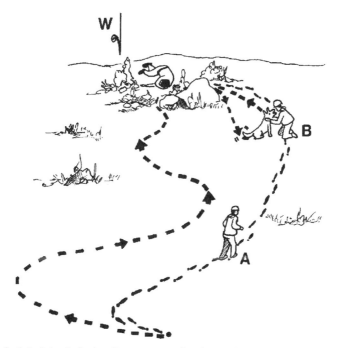

Recall/Refind: At Point A, the handler encourages his dog to close in on the alert. At Point B, the handler praises the dog for returning. The handler then accompanies and encourages the dog on the refind. *Linda Warshaw*

VARIATIONS

Apply these variations for Step 6:

1. Try the problems in an area approximately half a square mile, where the victim's location is unknown to you.

2. As the dog gets better, have the victim become progressively less responsive until the dog will indicate a "dead" victim. Alternate between responsive and unresponsive victims. The dog must understand that, no matter what, he must take you back to what he has found—even if it is a pair of unsuspecting lovers.

3. Do not use a scent article every time. Any human scent should be checked out and praised, even if it is not the correct one (to the dog, *all* human scent should be "correct").

4. Include short interruptions, including water breaks or meeting other handlers. Be friendly, but do not allow the dog to play during breaks. As soon as the short break is over, start out again in a businesslike manner. (There are many short interruptions on real missions.)

5. Try some night problems. This is the real test of your recall/refind. Since you, as a handler, have such poor night vision, you will have to rely heavily on your dog. Start in open fields and progress to light brush.

6. Try victims in different positions—up a tree, walking, standing, sitting, etc.—scent patterns will differ. Without such variations, dogs can become oriented only to victims who lie flat on the ground

7. Start working sectors adjacent to another dog and handler. Try to encounter other handlers and dogs occasionally so that the dogs get used to working with other dogs and handlers in the vicinity.

SCHEDULE
Follow this schedule for Step 6:

- Three to four times each session
- Two to three times a week

WHEN TO GO TO NEXT STEP
The dog will be ready to move to Step 7 when:

- He will lead you to the victim's location (unknown to you) at least 80 percent of the time.
- He leads you to the victim 90 percent of the time despite the fact you have veered off at least once.
- He can locate a victim at night 80 percent of the time.

Step 7: Testing and Polishing Search Skills

This is your final preparation for a real search mission. By practicing the following variations, you can consistently test yourself and your dog in all kinds of situations to find how well you are doing.

1. Do almost all problems where the victim's location is unknown to you.

2. Vary the length of the problems and the use of scent articles.

3. Practice very difficult terrain: heavy brush, large boulders, steep slopes. Start with half-hour problems, then work up to problems that last three or more hours.

4. Try trail running (hasty search) problems where the dog will indicate someone hidden off to the side of a road or trail. Some dogs hate to leave a well-beaten path to plow through the brush.

5. Try several varied terrain problems lasting four hours or more (take short breaks). Use two victims for the first and second time. Plan to find one near the beginning and one near the end of that time. If the dog works well after the second problem, use only one victim.

6. Gradually increase the dog's working time by starting with a one-hour problem. Rest the dog for half an hour or so and then work another one-hour problem. Eventually you will have a dog who will work all day.

7. Take another person with you so the dog is not distracted by having an entourage (on searches you will frequently have at least one other person with you). Keep the other person close behind you and downwind.

8. Try problems in extremes of weather:

   Heavy drizzle: Work grids very close together and find out at what distance the dog can detect victims.

   Poor wind: Test detection distance.

   Heat: Travel slowly and find how well the dog is paying attention with his nose, even when he looks tired. Keep the dog well watered and give him a chance to stabilize his panting every so often (heavy panting interferes with scenting).

9. Test your judgment of wind and terrain and the dog's ability to move in on faint scents. A polished search dog will recognize and work a faint scent, thereby requiring fewer passes and less time to search a sector. Start with field problems in a good breeze and know the approximate location of the victim. Estimate where you expect the dog to detect the air scent. Start approximately 200 feet further downwind from your estimated detection zone and run close grids back and forth until the dog picks up the scent. Alternate these problems with the exercise that follows, until you are quite accurate at gauging wind conditions.

10. Take a well-defined area and try very wide sweeps to see if the dog can pick up the scent. Make use of natural breaks in the terrain and natural wind funnels. This is called a *hasty search*. If you do not succeed, repeat the search in a more systematic pattern.

11. Try to intersect the last part of the victim's track and have the dog track or trail the victim approximately 100 to 200 feet to her location (be sure to cue the dog with a scent article). If the dog fails to respond, do not insist or force him. Complete the problem by going to systematic search sweeps.

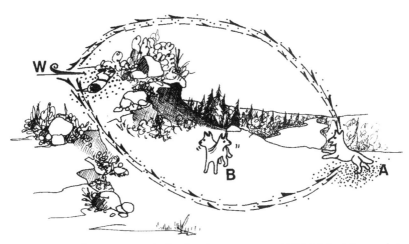

Learning scent diffusion: At Point A, the dog alerts on a scent. At Point B, he is in a pocket where no scent exists (due to diffusion by the knoll). Handlers must allow their dogs to range on either side of obstructions so the dog can recover the scent. *Linda Warshaw*

Dogs should learn to indicate articles. These house slippers were indicated by a dog just before he found the victim's body. *Penny Sullivan*

12. Leave a jacket or some other article in the search area for the dog to indicate, both as practice on indicating clues and to provide a motivational opportunity.

13. Have someone set up several problems for you in unfamiliar areas.

14. Work problems that have another dog and handler working an adjacent area.

Trail problem: X marks the spot where the dog should hit scent in a 15 mph breeze, if the victim (V) is in place for at least 20 minutes. *Linda Warshaw*

15. Work problems in areas that have some cows and/or horses. The dog should learn to leave them alone once he has acknowledged their presence.

Most of your training depends on how well your dog is doing and whether there is a need to backtrack occasionally and improve on his motivation. As you keep your dog in practice for searches, continue to try variations of all the above steps.

REMINDERS

Expect to have a few failures. If you have never had the experience of missing a victim, your training is not complete. Your problems may be too simple or you may be using areas that are too familiar.

It's a good idea—even a practical necessity—to take a two- or three-week break from training. Both dog and handler can then return refreshed and enthusiastic, especially if past training has been regular and consistent.

If training has been sporadic, it will naturally take longer to reach Step 7. You may find it necessary to cram four to six intensive, short working sessions close together to keep your dog from backsliding.

Somewhere along the way you should have completed your obedience class. All obedience lessons should be put to regular use. Remember that at the scene of a

MAINTAINING YOUR SEARCH DOG'S SKILLS

Once your dog has completed the search training outlined in Steps 1 through 7, you will need to keep his skills polished by practicing the following skill work:

- Concentrate on special skills, such as ladder climbing and the exercises described in disaster work.

- Improve ranging (when the dog works out ahead of his handler) by using shorter more frequent problems to produce a ranging dog.

- Check out old buildings and culverts, etc.

- Search for objects around and in the house (use the Look for it article-search command).

- Practice in contaminated suburban areas and around schools or shopping areas (during off hours).

- Learn elementary avalanche and disaster work techniques, even if you do not expect to use them. (You never know.)

Work your dog on some type of nose problem at least once each week (for example, finding a particular stick with your scent on it in a large woodpile or practicing a short neighborhood search).

A well-seasoned dog with two to three years of training can go a month or more without having a good search problem, but he should always have attention and some kind of "nose games." This type of month-long dry spell should be followed by three to four 30-minute to one-hour problems over a two-week period to keep the dog from becoming rusty. The only way to be sure your dog is kept in trim is by working him regularly.

Ideally, your dog is a house dog who spends 50 percent or more of his time in and around the house or traveling with you. Dogs who are kenneled rarely spend enough time with their handlers to develop the rapport necessary to travel to strange places and work long hours together. Even when he is not being trained, a house dog will be in a learning situation that keeps him alert and engaged (for example, behaving when guests are present, learning to play with the cat, not begging at the table and standing still for grooming). These occasions teach dogs to recognize the subtleties of human moods and normal human commotion. They will definitely give him a more well-rounded personality.

search your dog will be in the public eye, and he must be seen as a well-trained obedience dog. ARDA has found that dogs with poor obedience backgrounds have limited value as search dogs. They have a definite stopping point and usually will not work beyond it—even though the victim may be close at hand. An obedient dog will go the extra distance because you asked—and he is usually more successful due to that extra effort.

At some point in the later stages of training, you should accustom your dog to riding in aircraft (both fixed-wing and helicopter). It's fairly common for rescue teams to be airlifted to searches. Dogs must learn to get on and off aircraft while the engines are running, to save time and fuel. Han-

Dogs must learn to indicate human scent in unusual places. *Vicki Wooters*

dlers need to learn safety procedures, including how to select landing sites in case of evacuation, and what the correct weight allowances are for various types of aircraft. This training can frequently be arranged through local military bases.

All learning experiences have initial periods of quick learning and response and then, suddenly, they may hit a plateau or even mildly regress. As a handler, you may be plunged into despair when your dog suddenly appears to forget half of what he knows or seems to be stuck at one level of training. We call these *learning plateaus*. Learning plateaus inevitably occur between the fourth and sixth week of obedience classes. In search training, you should expect two such plateaus. The first plateau is likely to appear somewhere around Step 5. This usually constitutes a learning plateau for the dog. The second plateau usually occurs in Step 7 and represents a learning plateau for the handler.

The first plateau is often solved by reverting back to simple, quick problems with the dog for about two weeks. Sometimes the solution is a two-week break from all training.

The second plateau usually involves a handler who can't read his dog accurately on longer—or more complex—problems. This can result when a handler suspects that his dog is goofing off, or when a handler thinks he knows better than his dog. In any case, this stage must be worked through (the various parts of Step 7) until the handler is confident that he knows precisely what his dog is doing 95 percent of the time (the remaining 5 percent is confirmed visually).

SCHEDULE
Follow this schedule for Step 7:

- One to several exercises each session, depending upon the specific exercises

- One to two sessions a week

- Use all variations for a period of 10 weeks

Problem Solving

As you progress through various training steps, you may encounter certain problems that indicate you are either progressing too fast or your dog lacks proper motivation. The following suggestions should help solve some common problems.

- **Your dog will not range. He works only 10 or 15 feet in front of you in all terrain, including open spaces.** This indicates a dog who lacks sufficient motivation and who is not really interested in searching. You need to go back to short, easy problems and focus on game playing. It may be advisable to stop all search training for at least two weeks and spend that time developing your dog's play drive. When your dog is playing well with you, have other unit members and strangers play with him. Do not start longer problems or use other people as victims until the dog plays well.

- **Your dog is not interested in playing with a ball or a stick.** If you selected a puppy or dog according to the tests recommended in this book, you should not have this problem. This is more likely to occur in older dogs who have never had extensive play sessions.

  Your voice inflection will play a critical role here, as the dog picks up on your enthusiasm. You cannot afford to be shy if you want a happy, playful dog. It is usually more successful to start with a ball—its bouncing, rolling action is likely to attract your dog's interest. Using an excited, happy voice, attract your dog's attention to the ball by holding it in your hand and making short, darting movements near the ground. When the dog is watching closely, release the ball and let it roll a short distance. If the dog goes after the ball, praise him even if he does not pick it up. Then try again. If your dog picks up the ball, praise him lavishly. Try one more time, then *quit*. You do not want to bore your dog just as he is showing some interest.

Many dogs respond best when they can catch a ball that is thrown to them—or when they can chase a ball bouncing high in the air. Try several different approaches with your dog. Repeat these until your dog shows real enthusiasm. Then gradually increase the distance you roll the ball. If you work during the day, the best play time is immediately after you get home, when your dog is most excited to see you. Use this excitement to your advantage.

If your dog shows no interest in a ball, try a stick or something else that he likes to chew on. Then follow the same steps as for the ball. Some dogs prefer tug-of-war or pursuit, with you chasing him to "get the toy." Either is acceptable, so long as your dog enjoys it. As with a ball, stop while your dog is having fun. Even a few moments of play are an accomplishment that can be built upon.

- Experiment. Use whatever turns your dog on. It is *not* recommended that you use a glove, however. You will be wearing gloves in cold weather and on disaster missions, and you do not want your dog biting at your hand trying to grab the glove.

- If necessary, go to an obedience class or trainer where your dog can be taught to retrieve. Such training should *not* be forced—you want an avid, happy retriever.

- A word of caution on ball play and obedience classes: Some obedience instructors use a rolling ball as a test of the Sit or Down-stay. If you are trying to turn your dog into a compulsive player, the last thing you want is to correct him for going after the ball. Politely ask to be excused from this exercise.

- **Your dog does not take off enthusiastically on the Find command, even though he plays with a stick or ball when he finds his victim.** This often happens when a dog has not yet made the connection between the word Find and the act of searching. This usually occurs at the transition from simple problems with visual cues to problems where the dog is asked to look for a person who hid before he was brought to the work area. During the early problem, the dog's attention is on the person running instead of what the handler says.

The handler should use the dog's name just before releasing him, to guarantee his attention when he is given the "find" command: "Barry, find him!" Reinforce this command enthusiastically when your dog closes in by saying, "Good dog! Find him!" If necessary, go back to a few runaway-type problems to increase your dog's excitement and ensure that he learns the Find command.

First aid is a critical part of handler training. *Bill Syrotuck*

7

Handler Standards and Equipment

If you were to compare search and rescue to painting a picture, the dog would be the brush and the handler the artist: One is a tool and the other directs its action. Without the skilled control of a trained artist, the brush is just an inanimate piece of wood. Likewise, without the direction of a skilled handler, a dog is only out for a walk in the woods.

Standards

No one should enter search and rescue without realizing that she faces months of hard training. A sloppy, half-trained handler is detrimental to her dog, her unit and the entire search and rescue community. ARDA tolerates no compromise of the standards we developed over years of experience. The handler who "doesn't need" to learn first aid or doesn't want to become self-sufficient in the wilderness has no place in an ARDA unit.

Handlers need to develop a keen sense of the outdoors. It is very important that they notice and recognize landmarks. Handlers must pay close attention to vegetation, weather and wind conditions and know that these will affect their—and their dog's—performance. Above all, they need to intimately know their dogs' reactions and be able to understand them to the finest degree. This is accomplished through practice, practice and more practice. A handler and dog only become a team when this high degree of performance is achieved.

Physical and mental competence and integrity are absolute necessities. It is not unusual for a dog/handler team to be responsible for covering a sector one mile wide by two miles long, regardless of terrain. It is often necessary to go without sleep and still cover this terrain. Handlers have to work at night in complete darkness with only a headlamp, bearing in mind that they may be looking for a body. The later the hour, the more unnerving this can be.

Handlers need a positive attitude. They should always think "I *will* find that person." A negative attitude can be communicated to the dog. No one can be absolutely sure where a lost person is—thus, each area must be thoroughly and conscientiously searched.

This chapter sets forth ARDA's standards for handlers. They are based on the philosophy that a handler's action should never jeopardize the life of a victim or the effectiveness of the mission.

ARDA developed stringent standards to ensure that each handler has sufficient training in a multitude of skills. Some of these skills are used on every mission; some may never be used. But all of these skills should be learned so that handlers are prepared for any emergency.

First Aid

Since it takes only a fraction of a second for a *search* to become a *rescue*, no one in search work should consider undertaking missions without undergoing extensive first-aid training. ARDA standards specifically require handlers to have the Red Cross Emergency Response training or its equivalent. Many ARDA handlers are emergency medical technicians (EMT). Although this level of training is not required for everyone, each unit should have at least one EMT.

Cardiopulmonary resuscitation (CPR) training is also highly recommended. Most importantly: a handler must be certified by the American Red Cross or an appropriate state agency. Certification not only guarantees a high level of training, but also supplies some protection in the event of a lawsuit.

On many missions, rescue squad personnel are standing by at the base camp. However, it may take them an hour to reach the victim's location. The victim may not be able to wait that long for medical attention. *You* must be prepared to stabilize the patient and perhaps help in his evacuation. First-aid courses teach basic transport of a patient to minimize further injury. Expect transport to be even more difficult in the woods. You may have a Stokes litter (a wire basket litter), but no backboard. You must know how to move an injured person from the ground into a Stokes and then transport that person without compounding any injuries. You must be able to organize and direct an evacuation, know how to select the safest yet quickest route out of the woods, be prepared to cut a path with a machete and know the correct way to carry a litter over uneven ground without causing undue discomfort to the patient. All this will require training and practice beyond the scope of most first-aid courses.

Handlers must practice medical evacuations in difficult terrain. *Penny Sullivan*

When taking first-aid classes, pay close attention to the types of injuries likely to occur in the woods: snakebites, allergic reactions to stings, broken limbs, burns (from campfires or stoves), cuts, abrasions, gunshot wounds (accidental or suicidal), heart attacks, strokes, diabetic reactions, etc. Lost people often suffer from medical problems, such as Alzheimer's, which may affect their behavior in the woods. With relatively young, healthy people—particularly hunters and hikers—injury is always a possibility. Falls are common—such as slipping off a cliff and landing on a ledge—and you must know how to treat victims who are suffering from a broken back or neck. Improper treatment could paralyze or even kill them.

The most frequent hazards in the out-of-doors are *shock* and *hypothermia*. Treat these immediately with all the warmth (inside and outside), rest and reassurance you can. More people die from shock and hypothermia than from any injury.

You can only be prepared for a few emergencies at a time. Anything disasterous requires a great deal of improvisation—and much more equipment than you can carry in your daypack. However, skilled first aid providers can handle a wide variety of emergencies with relatively limited supplies.

The equipment every handler should carry in the field includes:

- **Sterile dressing:** large, heavy compress with ties (try to get one in a can or a waterproof wrap).

- **Band-aids (four to six):** good sticky ones for minor personal injuries; when pulled snugly across a laceration or gash it will usually stop bleeding as well.

An ARDA handler administers to an elderly man who was found by ARDA dogs. *Emil Pelcak*

- **Elastic bandage, three inches wide:** serves a variety of purposes, from holding a dressing to splinting.

- **Aspirin or Acetominephin (12):** a generally safe medication with moderate pain relief (mostly for personal use).

- **Safety pins (two to four):** serves a variety of purposes.

- **Metal mirror:** its clear surface is used to check for moisture to see if a victim is breathing; also used for signaling.

- **"Space blanket":** used to cover shock or hypothermia victim to help retain body heat.

- **Bouillon cubes or instant soup (in paper packet):** provides hot liquids to help warm a *conscious* hypothermia victim. Always carry either a metal cup or metal canteen so it can be used to heat the water.

- **Snakebite and allergy kits, as needed.**

Be sure to keep all items clean and neat in plastic wrappers.

You are accepting a huge responsibility by volunteering to look for someone in trouble. You must be prepared to handle it.

Map and Compass

A dog, a radio, a map and a compass: Any one without the others will render you virtually useless. The dog is your reason for being present; the radio is your link to the outside world; the map and compass determine the accuracy and ultimate success of your effort.

TOPOGRAPHICAL MAPS

A topographical ("topo") map serves many purposes. First, it determines your primary search area (when combined with information on the missing person) and sector breakdowns, based on existing or arbitrary boundaries. Second, it records the progress of the search based on areas covered and provides planning data for expanded coverage. You cannot conduct a professional, accurate search without a topo map (using a 7.5 minute or 1:24,000 map is recommended because it details such things as power lines, dirt roads, trails, marshes, etc.).

ARDA requires "intimate knowledge" of topographical maps, and means just that. Every member of your unit must be extremely proficient with both the map and compass—base camp personnel included. ARDA recommends Bjorn Kjellstrom's *Be Expert with Map and Compass* (American Orienteering Service, 1967) as a textbook. Other sources of instruction include local orienteering clubs, a nearby national park that offers orienteering courses, or past or present members of the military.

ORIENTEERING

Orienteering courses teach the basics of using a compass. Orienteering competitions are based on point-to-point compass work over a prescribed course and against the clock. Various markers are set along a course and must be reached in a specific order. Although your compass work on a search may not be as precise as the orienteering course, the training is a must. You will be able to do precise work if it is ever necessary. (For example, you may be asked to check an old house site in the middle of the woods and must go directly there from base camp.)

On searches, compass work is much more general. You will set your compass bearing (direction of travel) along one of your boundaries—based upon wind conditions and your search plan—then follow that general bearing to your next boundary instead of a particular marker. If you work your initial boundary correctly and assess the wind well, your dog's nose will cover the area that you do not physically walk through. When you reach your far boundary, you will turn and follow it for whatever distance you think will ensure the dog's detection of anyone between your sweeps. Your passes may be less than 100 feet if there is no wind, or up to 300 feet apart if there is a good breeze. Vegetation also determines the width of your sweeps. Once you make a decision, you will turn and work parallel to your original path, using your compass to direct you. Again, you will be working to a boundary rather than a specific point. Even though you will be working boundary-to-boundary rather than point-to-point, an orienteering course will give you a firm foundation in the use of the map and compass.

On searches where no topo map is available, handlers have to rely solely on their compasses and must be prepared to draw a detailed map of their area when they return to base. To prepare for this, handlers must remember and note major terrain features and their path through the sector. This takes a great deal of practice and a real familiarity with map drawing. The best way to master this skill is to have handlers draw maps of their training problems, even if they have topo maps. They should also practice tracing or drawing their sector from the base map, for those instances on real searches when an individual copy for each handler is not available.

Handlers should practice without a map, using only their compass. They should also practice with no compass, using only terrain features as their guide. Night searches should be practiced, since the loss of long-range visibility forces greater reliance on the compass. An excellent training exercise is a night orienteering course; a handler who can work such a precision course at night will have no trouble with a night search. Working a strange woods at night is a real test of a handler's skill—and night searches are as common as daylight searches. Failure to do night searches because handlers lack map and compass skills means failure to do the best job for the victim.

While the development of Global Positioning Satellite (GPS) technology can prove extremely helpful to search and rescue workers, it should not be the sole

Every unit member must be extremely proficient with a map and compass. Peggy Williams

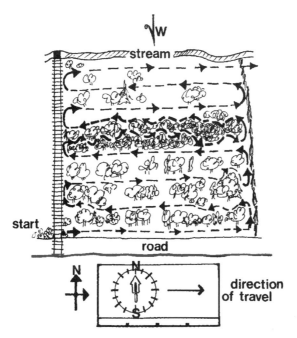

Use your compass bearing (direction of travel) to go from boundary to boundary, varying sweep widths to accommodate changes in terrain or vegetation. *Linda Warshaw*

land navigational tool for dog handlers. Every handler must be required to meet the map and compass standards, even if hand-held GPS instruments are available.

Likewise, grid-line search techniques—where handlers only feel secure if others are within a few hundred feet on either side of them—reflect a unit that doesn't use its teams to their best advantage. This method greatly reduces the working scope of each dog, defeats the purpose of search dog units (to cover large areas rapidly and effectively with minimum manpower) and creates unnecessary interference from nearby dogs and handlers.

Units should not begin taking on searches until all handlers are capable of working independently— day or night—in any terrain. The role of the map and compass is too critical to approach them with a haphazard attitude. Handler training in this aspect must be thorough.

Base camp operators must also learn their responsibilities relevant to the use of the map and compass. Base should have some type of map table or board and a clear plastic overlay upon which a felt-tip marker can be used for notations.

The base operator will need to mark the following on the overlay:

- The victim's point last seen

- Each sector boundary and unit number of the assigned handler

- Any changes to information on the map (new logging roads, etc.)

- Any alerts or clues reported by handlers

- Areas covered by other resources

- The base camp location

- The exact route of the handlers through their sectors

All of the above can be practiced while handlers train in sector searching and during mock searches.

Survival

ARDA's survival philosophy expects handlers to be able to support themselves, their dogs and the victim for up to 24 hours if evacuation is delayed due to weather, darkness or terrain. The required equipment must be lightweight yet dependable.

Handlers must be prepared to build a fire, build a shelter and provide food and drink for themselves, their dogs and the victim. As previously noted, handlers must also carry first-aid equipment.

Survival equipment includes:

- **Knife:** A heavy-duty, Swiss-Army type with multiple blades and accessories is ideal. You may have to cut heavy branches for shelter, for firewood or to make a splint.

- **Matches (waterproof and windproof):** Must be carried in a waterproof container; do not use your matches for lighting cigarettes.

- **Rope (about 50 feet, ⅛-inch nylon):** May be used to help your dog down a cliff, tie a tarp to branches for shelter, or as shoelaces, etc.

- **Wire or folding saw:** Used to cut firewood, splints, stretcher poles, etc.

- **Whistle (low pitch and loud):** Supplies directional help to bring evacuation assistance or in case your radio fails.

- **Water purification tablets or kit:** Used to purify water from question- able water sources.

- **Canteen:** Should be metal or have a metal cup so it can be used to heat water. Refill your canteen with fresh water each day before leaving base camp and top off at every opportunity.

- **Firestarter:** Commercial items available for starting fires when kindling is damp.

- **Plastic tarp (9-x-12-foot):** Supplies shelter.

- **Flares (day and night):** Used for signaling helicopters, base camp, noting the victim's location, etc.; flares must be used with extreme caution due to fire danger.

- **Food:** Enough for you, your dog and the victim. This should include at least one emergency meal (freeze-dried), instant soups, high-energy snacks and patties for the dog.

The unit should be instructed in using improvised gear for overnight survival. They should also be taught to identify edible foods that are available in the woods. Each unit member should practice setting up a survival camp during an overnight training session.

Equipment

First-aid and survival equipment have already been covered. In addition, there are many other personal items that each member must have. Rather than rushing out and buying everything at once, handlers should gradually purchase these items as their training progresses and they determine what best suits their needs.

RADIO

The radio is a critical lifeline between handlers, base camp and any necessary additional medical or agency assistance. It is absolutely essential that all teams have radios when they participate in real searches. Since a radio can be an expensive item, it is advisable to make this one of the first unit purchases. The unit as a whole should discuss radio communications and the feasibility of different types of radios.

- **Citizens' Band (CB):** CB units are popular and fairly inexpensive. The main advantage here is cost. The main disadvantages to CBs are crowded channels, the number of people who will overhear your conversations and the limited range.

- **Business and Public Safety Band (FM):** These units are more expensive than CBs, but have advantages of range, power supply, frequency assignment and a smaller, more flexible antenna. Business and Public Safety Band radios require special licenses and are used by police, fire and rescue squad personnel.

- **Amateur Radio:** This could be a consideration, although the equipment is relatively expensive and each member would need a license.

A communications officer should be appointed to investigate the various radio systems and required licensing. This person will also be responsible for radio maintenance and communications training within the unit.

Radio communications should be practiced at each unit workout. If you are to be regarded as a professional, you must act and *sound* professional. Each unit member should be well-versed in radio procedures under Federal Communications Commission rules and regulations, while base operators are expected to exhibit an above-average knowledge of these procedures.

All members must have training in basic field trouble-shooting. This includes changing batteries and replacing antennas. Each handler must be prepared to use a click code in case their radio transmits sounds but not voices. Base camp, upon realizing such a problem, should ask a series of questions that can be answered by clicks that signify "yes" or "no." Your radio is too important to lose because of minor problems that handlers should be able to overcome.

Radio conversations interrupt the concentration of dogs and handlers. Each dog and handler must learn to continue as though no interruption has occurred. As soon as a unit has both base and hand-held radios, they must begin practice so that radio communication becomes second nature.

Both handlers and base personnel must be prepared to survive in any climate. ARDA handlers are shown here with backpacks containing gear necessary to support themselves, their dogs and the victim. *Jeff Doran*

DEVELOPING UNIT CODES

Unit codes should be developed to ensure the privacy of communications. Codes should include:

- A number for each unit member.
- The condition of the subject (alive and well, alive but ill/injured or deceased).
- Finding clues.
- Handler operations (beginning and ending sectors, status check).
- A code should also be developed so that the base camp operator can warn handlers to stifle any transmissions if an unauthorized person is near the radio.

CLOTHING AND FIELD GEAR

The unit should decide upon the uniform that every member wears on a search. Wearing uniforms makes a group look professional and also makes each member identifiable to the agency.

- **Uniform.** Choose your uniform with visibility, and safety (you don't want to wear camouflage during hunting season) in mind. Uniforms should include identifying insignia, such as unit patches.

- **Shirt.** Shirts should have long sleeves that can be rolled up during hot daytime hours and rolled down during cool evening hours. It is best to wear cotton in warm weather and wool in cold weather.

- **Trousers.** Trousers should be long (for protection), snagproof, wind resistant and loose fitting (for easy movement and good circulation). Hunters' "brush" or "bush" pants are useful because the nylon front enables briers to slide right over them. However, they can be hot in the summer. In winter, extra pants should be worn underneath them.

- **Jacket.** The best kind of jacket is a water-resistant mountain parka. These parkas are also snagproof and windproof. They should be in a highly visibile color, such as international orange.

- **Boots.** Boots must be heavy duty, lightweight, and equipped with nonslip soles. Use waterproof leather. Plain or simulated rubber is dangerous in cold weather or snow. Snow packs are ideal for winter or wet and cold conditions.

Handlers should carry a plastic tarp for emergency shelter. *Penny Sullivan*

- **Hat**. A hardhat is required in the woods for safety purposes, and when flying on military aircraft (a chin strap is also required). A hardhat can also be used to give your dog water.

- **Rain Gear.** Suitable rain gear includes durable pants and jackets. These should be in a highly visibile color and should fit over other clothing. Ponchos do not work well, because they leak and snag easily.

- **Underjacket:** Most units use these under parkas, which are rarely warm enough. Experienced outdoorsmen know that the best protection against cold and hypothermia is layered clothing, so layers can be added or removed depending on changes in temperature.

- **Gloves:** Good leather gloves are required for protection and are particularly necessary for disaster missions.

- **Socks:** Socks should be made of light wool, or cotton with a second pair of heavy wool.

- **Personal pack:** This will be left at base. The pack should include extra socks, a wool sweater, extra shirts and pants, undergarments, lightweight shoes, personal hygiene items, a good-quality sleeping bag—rated to at least -20°F, with pad—stove/fuel/personal eating utensils, and a two-person tent (for you and your dog).

- **Personal field pack:** This should be a fanny pack or something similar that can be used in the field. The personal field pack will contain the previously listed first-aid and survival supplies, as well as a headlamp

with batteries, spare compass (liquid-filled), adhesive tape, insect repel-
lent, paper and pencil, disposable towelettes, aluminum foil, toilet paper,
surveyor's flagging tape, heat packs, extra flashlight bulbs and batteries,
and a camera with extra film.

Specific conditions in your region will dictate additions or deletions from this
list. However, each person must carry enough equipment to handle any emergency
likely to occur. All items for the personal field pack can easily fit into a well-made
beltbag or fanny pack. Hours of working in rough terrain and weather require handlers to carry as much as possible with as little weight as possible. Each item in
this list has been selected because it meets this requirement.

All your gear must be readily packed into a flyaway or duffel bag in the event
your unit is airlifted to a search. Aircraft are limited in the weight they can carry,
so unit members must know the combined weight of themselves, their dogs and
their gear.

*To become a well-equipped, well-trained handler requires months of
hard work—and no small amount of personal expense. Once you
begin taking searches, however, you will appreciate all the extra time
and effort you put into preparing to join a group that can handle any
required task.*

An ARDA evaluator checks off equipment as a unit member goes through his field pack.
Penny Sullivan

A central coordinating number enables agencies to contact ARDA through the River Vale, New Jersey, Police Department. *Courtesy of River Vale, New Jersey, Police Department*

8

The Search Dog Unit

Once your unit has gone active and made a commitment to your local area to engage in search and rescue activities, it must stand behind its commitment. Therefore, it is essential that the unit be fully trained and equipped to meet its responsibilities at all times. The confidence of official agencies responsible for searches will have to be earned by the unit's competence and professionalism.

Be Ready to Respond

When a search situation arises, the unit must respond. Answers such as, "It's too late," "It's too cold," "It's too far away," "We don't have any dogs available" or "No one wants to go" can't be tolerated. The only correct answer to a request for assistance is, "Where and when do we meet?"

Units must be prepared to respond to an average of three calls—with the possibility of 10 to 15—a month. At least one operational leader (OL) and three other members should be prepared to leave their homes or places of employment within one hour of a call.

Operational leaders should always be prepared for the worst possible type of search mission in their area. They should also maintain their unit in a state of readiness for this type of situation. That way, when it occurs, the unit's performance will reflect the high standard of excellence that the group has tried so hard to achieve.

Units must always be professional. Members should know exactly what to do and then do it with confidence. Since the dogs will catch the eye of the public and the news media, it is imperative they reflect a high level of training.

In short, if a unit cannot fulfill the responsibility of an active search organization, it should not become active.

ORGANIZING YOUR UNIT

The preliminary structure of each unit should consist of people (the minimum number of which is given later in this chapter) who have a strong interest in forming a search unit and who have had some dog training experience. They should also have a sound outdoor and camping background.

Within each unit, two leadership structures are necessary—one for administering the organization and one for search operations. In small units, these jobs may be combined. Organizational leadership should include elected officers (a president, vice president, secretary and treasurer), who are responsible for the day-to-day management of the unit's business.

For search operations, an operational leader should be elected from the group. Doing so ensures the respect and cooperation of all unit members. The operational leader should determine the availability of search management courses, and participate in one or more courses, as this is a complex skill requiring specialized training.

A unit's success or failure rests on the shoulders of its leaders, as does the responsibility to see that each topic discussed here is carried out. Of course some responsibilities should be delegated to other unit members, but the group's leaders should be fully versed on each subject.

COOPERATION

Unit members are responsible for cooperating with their leaders. They should be prepared to spend a considerable amount of time training their dogs and themselves. The unit depends on teamwork. Failure of one person on the team reflects on the entire unit—and may possibly influence the unit's ultimate success or failure. For example, a search area may be reported "clear." If, at a later date, the lost person is located dead within this so-called "cleared" area by other means, one can be certain the dog group will never be asked to search that jurisdiction again. Not only does this failure reflect on the group, but it also reflects on the value of search dogs in general.

MINIMUM NUMBER OF DOG TEAMS
AND LENGTH OF TRAINING

Once it is established that a group meets the necessary requirements, it should proceed to organize in each area outlined in this chapter. The group should not rely on the availability of just two or three dogs. The ideal minimum number to start with is six or more highly trained dogs and handlers. The hazard of relying

Handlers must learn to work together to ensure the search is well-coordinated and that all areas are covered. *Emil Pelcak*

upon only a few dogs is that one dog may become injured or unavailable and the remaining one or two dogs may be unable to respond on a search that day. In this case, the absence of just one dog leaves the unit's efficiency at a low level. A second consideration is having enough dogs and handlers to carry out two or more searches at one time.

On the basis of the information in this chapter, each unit should train for at least one year. One of the greatest hazards to search work is a unit that commits itself too soon.

Preliminary Research

Each prospective search and rescue unit should make a careful survey of their local area to determine the types of situations in which they may be expected to help. The following topics must all be considered.

SUBJECT OF SEARCH

Various types of individuals may be involved:

- **Aged:** senior citizens who have become disoriented in wooded areas.

- **Adults:** hikers, hunters, etc., who have become lost or injured and have not returned at a predetermined time.

- **Teenagers:** they may become lost due to a variety of reasons.

- **Children:** small children who have wandered away from campgrounds or homes adjacent to wooded areas.

- **Evasives:** mental patients who hide because they do not want to be found; children who hide because of the fear of punishment; suicide victims who have indicated their intention but have not yet committed the act—many go into wooded areas to commit suicide and do not want to be found.

The subjects outlined above present different types of behavior. These behaviors should be tabulated for future reference so the unit can anticipate the appropriate areas to search and the response of the individual. (See the Appendix for more about the behavior of lost persons.) Obviously, an evasive who is running away behaves quite differently from a hunter who runs toward you with joy at being found.

CONDITION OF VICTIM

Your unit must also be aware of the various physical conditions in which victims may be found and be prepared to handle each. Below are some of the conditions in which a victim may be found:

- **Exposure (hypothermia):** subject has inadequate protection against the elements.

- **Broken bones:** subject falls over a cliff or breaks an ankle.

- **Shock:** can be caused by a variety of reasons.

- **Unconsciousness:** can be caused by a variety of reasons.

- **Dead**

TERRAIN

The types of terrain should be considered and tabulated, because different types of terrain affect the ability of the dog and handler as well as the subject of the search. Terrain types include mountainous (below tree line), marshland (wooded plus watered areas), heavily wooded (trees very close together), and forested (wooded and open areas). Subjects will take different courses of action relative to the terrain. In mountainous areas, hunters tend to follow drainages. Evasives tend to cross marshy areas to evade tracking dogs.

The terrain has an impact on how each dog team works. Mountains affect scent flow, as well as the handler's ability to maneuver; marshlands can have vast, impassable areas of water; heavily wooded areas often have very little scent flow and briars or dense brush can prevent a handler from thoroughly covering the area. The well-trained, experienced dog/handler team learns to compensate for most of these problems, however.

CLIMATE AND WEATHER

Climate is very important in determining a dog's ability to scent. Factors to consider include: sunshine (hot days—above 90°F), rain (downpours or showers), snow (heavy or light), cold (below 0°F); humidity (coastal regions), and dryness (desert areas). A unit in one area of the country may approach a search problem quite differently than another, even though both units may be looking for the same type of victim.

TIME OF YEAR

Since some dogs may initially refuse to work under certain adverse conditions, they should be conditioned to work in any of the four seasons: winter (rain or snow), spring (a change in vegetation), summer (climate relative to area), fall (rain, a change in vegetation).

TIME OF DAY

Both dogs and handlers must be prepared to work during any part of the day or night. Handlers should be aware of the different wind conditions and climate variations that may occur in the same area, and how they may change between morning and night.

AREA

Different parts of a state, such as mountains or wooded areas, will have higher loss rates than, for example, urban areas. Wooded areas draw hunters, while mountainous areas draw hikers. These areas should be well plotted. Research is important because it gives a unit the ability to simulate the types of searches common to its area. Information can be gathered from sheriff departments' or state agencies' records (such as those in the Department of Emergency Services), newspapers or records of other units. Research should go back at least three years and information should be tabulated in a meaningful manner. Final data should show what the unit must be prepared for and what it should practice during workouts. Obviously, there are many different combinations, but with good statistics a unit is better able to predict and handle any situation.

With these statistics, a unit can practice the most common occurrences. They can reconstruct various situations and try different types of solutions.

In general, the unit should concentrate its training on:

- Both day and night practices
- Various weather conditions

- Changes in terrain
- Lengthening practice times (dogs should eventually work eight to twelve hours)

Research will dictate the type of training each unit should undergo for both dogs and handlers. If a unit tries to simulate actual conditions by conducting mock searches from time to time, it won't be caught unprepared.

SPECIAL CONDITIONS

Each unit should also consider any special conditions unique to their location. For example, if your area is prone to earthquakes or hurricanes, your unit might consider specialized training in disaster response.

Discipline

Along with cooperation from its members, each unit also requires discipline. Both cooperation and discipline are necessary in training—and especially in the field during actual searches.

If a practice session is called for every other weekend, unit members should try to attend all sessions. This would constitute only 25 sessions, but it takes a considerable amount of time. In a sense, the effort of attending sessions can be considered self-discipline.

Group discipline is also necessary because groups establish unity through discipline. Once basic policies have been decided on, all unit members should adhere to them, as well as to the assignments of the OL. Occasionally, individuals have their own ideas and exercise them. Glory hunters, interested only in their own success, sometimes deliberately leave their own area and cross into that of others, convinced the victim is there. The hazard, of course, is that the victim won't be found by the glory hunter, who will both have left his assigned area unsearched and compromised the area of another handler.

A saying used by responsible agencies is: "If a member commits an error through ignorance, this indicates poor training; if the error is committed knowingly, this indicates poor discipline." Responsible agencies do not deal with all the members of a unit. They deal with the unit's OL, who is ultimately responsible for the unit's performance—and therefore has the final reprimand. All members should know that errors reflect upon the group leadership and the unit as a whole.

Discipline must be practiced during the training phase. In addition, regular meetings should be held to give group members an opportunity to air their ideas. Leaders should be willing to consider and discuss new ideas. Once an idea has been accepted or rejected, the group must adhere to the final decision.

Deportment

Discipline ensures that an order is carried out, but deportment concerns *how* the order is carried out. It is important for the unit to achieve and maintain a professional attitude and appearance.

- All members should wear appropriate clothing: good boots with Vibram soles, and a suitable unit uniform.

- All members should know their functions to avoid confusion, misunderstandings or arguments. If an OL makes a request, the group member should carry it out quietly and efficiently. Disagreements should be aired privately later.

- Everyone should be busy and look as though they have a job, whether it's preparing their own gear or helping out someone else. Don't stand around and talk; searches and training sessions are not social encounters.

Good training should keep unit members from panicking in most situations. A unit's first successful find can be a memorable event—do not turn it into a catastrophe. There have been occasions where, in their excitement, unit members don't remember their radio call sign. In their anxiety, their voices become higher than normal, their speech garbled, and the entire context of the message rendered meaningless.

Only operational leaders should confer with the search director. Avoid situations where the whole group descends upon the director to voice their opinion on solving the problem. Neither OLs nor members should ever imply that a search is being mishandled.

Your unit should avoid making demands of responsible agencies or leaders. If your group has not been called early enough, try your best anyway.

Your unit should avoid making excuses. In training sessions, if a dog is not working or a handler commits an error, accept it and learn from it. You cannot make excuses on a real search—someone's life may be at stake.

Getting along with others is a basic criterion. The unit system requires teamwork. If one person antagonizes other members instead of working toward unity, the group may become

A unit coordinator takes down information on an incoming search call. *Penny Sullivan*

separated through anger. Handlers in the field experience many hardships, and the OL will push teams to the limit. It takes very little to produce unrest, unless everyone pulls together.

Developing a Unit Notification System

Once the unit has reached a state of proficiency and feels ready to take on real missions, it must develop a coordinating system whereby handlers can be quickly notified of an impending mission. This is especially true in avalanche or disaster work.

There are several methods by which this notification process can be accomplished:

- One coordinator can be established to receive incoming calls from the agency and, in turn, quickly notify unit members of the mission. This coordinator must be 100 percent accessible, either by telephone, cell phone or pager. The quickest way to lose a search is if an agency can't reach you in one or two phone calls.

  If agencies have one phone number to call, it makes it easier— and more efficient —to get in touch with your unit. The coordinator receives the incoming call, obtains an elementary description of the type of mission and records the caller's name and phone number. The coordinator then contacts the unit's operational leader and takes instructions on who to call, along with any other specific instructions.

- Another coordinating system involves using a single telephone number. However, once contact has been made duties are subdivided to other designated persons. The first coordinator informs two other subcoordinators, each of whom have specific numbers to call. Consequently, two coordinators work together at the same time. This system is twice as fast as the others, but the need for such a system depends on the size of the unit. In a unit with 20 to 30 members, everyone can be contacted quickly. If there are only 10 unit members, a single coordinator may suffice.

- If there is no single coordinator, the unit can provide a list of numbers to the agency. If there is no answer at the first number, the agency then calls each number in sequence. Units must establish a duty roster that ensures one of the phone numbers is manned at all times. Once contact has been made with a unit member, the procedure is the same as in the first example. This system is less desirable, since agencies end up wasting precious time calling four or five numbers.

For brief intervals when telephones are unmanned, an answering machine should be used. Answering machines—or voice mail—can record messages or inform callers of the next number to phone. Call-forwarding can also be used to automatically forward calls to a manned number.

Coordinating systems are needed to facilitate rapid notification of handlers. The more efficient the system, the more efficient the unit.

Coordinating a Mission

On receiving a call, the unit coordinator should gather the following information:

1. Subject category (elderly, hunter, etc.).

2. Length of time the search has already been in progress.

3. Weather conditions under which the handlers will be working.

4. Type of terrain to be searched and if a topographical map of the area is available.

5. Any special considerations.

Items one and two are straightforward. Item three is important to a centrally based unit. Knowing something about the environment helps unit members select proper clothing and equipment. During rain and damp weather, handlers are advised against using goosedown clothing. Snow and higher altitudes call for good wool or down clothing, snowshoes or skis and adequate changes of clothing. Searching in very hot weather requires cotton or light wool. It is vital that the coordinator find out what circumstances the unit is getting into.

Knowledge about the terrain helps to determine what type of equipment to have on hand. Handlers working snow slopes should use ice axes, snowshoes and crampons. Sometimes this same gear can be used in rocky terrain. All units should consider maintaining snow gear, since approximately 75 percent of the United States receives significant snowfall.

Environments and terrain can change from one extreme to the other on search and rescue missions in the United States. Units have to decide where they will work. They may take on any and all types of missions. If so, units need to be prepared for the rigors of Mount McKinley in the winter and Death Valley in the summer. Handlers will need wardrobes that will protect them against weather extremes; have the equipment to handle a range of environments and the knowledge to survive and work in extreme surroundings.

Interviewing people found by your unit will add to your research on victim behavior. *Emil Pelcak*

If your unit limits itself to specific missions, you should know what other unit can handle a mission beyond your scope and then refer that unit to the requesting agency. Units and handlers should not attempt missions beyond their capability. By the same token, don't be afraid to attempt something new. Advise the agency of what you estimate the possibilities to be and state that you are willing to try.

Units must be prepared to set up base camp in remote locations where self-sufficiency is required. *Bill Syrotuck*

9

Unit Training

There are two main purposes for unit workouts: to set up problems for each dog, and to exercise the unit in synchronizing a search for one victim. The unit should either alternate each workout to accommodate each purpose or accomplish both at the same workout, depending upon the needs of the unit.

Workout Schedules

Workouts are scheduled one or two times a month throughout the year. Small groups made up of people who live near one another can work together between times, as long as beginning handlers are thoroughly briefed on training procedures. New units often schedule weekly sessions, particularly until they are fully operational. Once operational, they may reduce their training to once or twice a month, with handlers working their dogs on motivational problems between unit training sessions.

Each unit must determine what schedule works best to accommodate the members' various levels of training. A person who is skilled at both dog and handler training should be appointed as training officer. It will be this individual's responsibility to schedule all workouts.

WORKOUT PROBLEMS

Good workouts require careful advance planning. Prepare your area so there is maximum work time for the dog, and minimum time to get the victim(s) in and out of place. Be sure to use good boundaries at first. You should have enough victims to go around. Use adults—not children—for problems that will last a long time.

- For individual dog problems, the "victim" should be thoroughly briefed on where to be and how to behave (play, lie still, talk, etc.) when found by the dog.

- Generally, advanced dog handlers *should not* know where their victim is located. Beginning dog handlers *should* know the general location of their victims most of the time. Intermediate dog handlers may know, depending on the training required.

- When each dog of the unit has an 80-percent success rate on individual problems, the training officer can start working them simultaneously on sector problems under simulated search conditions. The training officer will place one victim in a large area. That area is divided into sectors and the dogs start searching. This should be practiced frequently, as each dog will have to be aware of the other dog's presence (even if he is a quarter mile away). When first practicing such a search problem, each dog who worked a sector with no victim should be given a short motivational find at the end.

- Use part of the time to teach base camp procedures and equipment, radio operations, checking on outdoor skills, navigation, evacuation techniques, group obedience and agility practice, and to test field gear and equipment.

- Workouts are never canceled due to weather. If roads are dangerous, use another area.

EVALUATION TESTS

An evaluation committee should be formed under the leadership of the training officer. It will be their responsibility to establish and administer tests that each dog/handler team must pass prior to becoming operational. These tests can be performed during scheduled unit workouts, with a written record kept of each test.

ARDA uses the following evaluation tests: open field, trail (hasty search), light brush, dense brush, night problem and multiple-victim problem. The test areas range from a trail one-half to one mile in length to an area one-quarter square mile (one-half mile long by one-half mile wide) or larger. Tests may last from one hour for the hasty search to six hours for the multiple-victim problem. The tests are designed to observe the eagerness, ranging, recall/refind and long-term working ability of the dog, as well as the handler's ability to use a map and compass, evaluate and physically handle a variety of terrain and read the dog.

Practicing Search Methods

The sector system, developed by SARDA after several years of research, should be the basis for all unit searching. Originally referred to as the "corridor system," ARDA changed the terminology in the 1970s because so many non-ARDA handlers incorrectly assumed "corridor" meant the dogs were to be used on a grid line with each spaced only a few hundred feet apart.

THE SECTOR SYSTEM

The sector system was developed because a search area is normally quite vast. It may encompass 360° from where a person stands and may extend several miles in any direction. At first glance, the area is overwhelming. The solution, therefore, is to subdivide the area into sectors and to assign a dog to each sector, with all searching simultaneously. The sectors are divided from one another by geographical features, such as ridges, drainages, roads, streams, etc., which define the boundaries. A dog and handler may then be responsible for the area bounded by two ridges and a stream or any other configuration that is easily recognizable.

For example, an area between two streams (approximately one mile apart) and bounded by a peak at the far end and a road at the near end (two miles apart) is assigned to one dog and handler. One mile from the stream that forms one boundary of the first sector is a power line running to the peak. A second sector is defined as the area between the power line and the stream common to the previous sector, the peak and the road. The second sector is assigned to a second dog and handler. Obviously, with six dogs the area can be divided into six sectors or the search area can be expanded with each working equally large areas.

The Importance of Teamwork

The most important part of sector searching is teamwork. Coordination is the responsibility of the operational leader, and radio communications are essential. The operational leader must know what is happening at all times and know the progress of each team. Each team must know the locations of the other teams and their progress. Inexperienced teams tend to continually find each other. This is due to several factors:

- Inability of the handlers to stay within their boundaries.

- Inability of the dogs to ignore fellow searchers.

- Handlers not keeping good radio contact and describing their progress.

- Handlers not watching their compass.

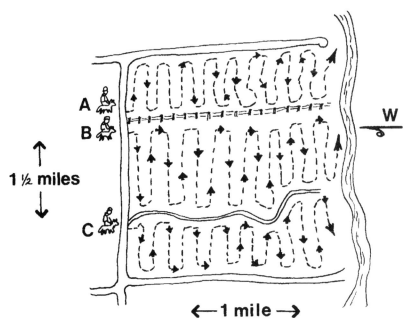

Obvious boundaries (fence, stream and road) should be used to divide sectors.
Linda Warshaw

An area between two streams, the peak and road is assigned to one handler (1). The area between the stream, power line, peak and road is assigned to the second handler (2).
Linda Warshaw

> *To ensure accuracy, all the skills required for sector searching must be constantly practiced at unit workouts.*

Before handlers can begin working sectors, they must understand how to use wind currents, terrain features and their map and compass. One of the best training techniques for new handlers is to accompany experienced handlers several times to observe how they subdivide and work their sectors. Periodically, experienced handlers should also accompany trainees to answer questions and provide guidance.

Following the Search Plan

Handlers should develop their search plan before leaving base, including setting the compass bearing they will follow. Once this basic plan is decided upon, only pronounced changes in weather or terrain should alter it. Changing a plan midsector may result in leaving large "holes" in coverage and greatly reducing the probability of finding the victim. However, some sectors contain such a variety of terrain (drainages, small knolls, etc.) that the same pattern cannot be applied throughout. In those cases, it would be advisable to subdivide the sector and work each feature with a different, more appropriate pattern.

When possible, sectors should be approached from a starting point near base. If the wind is coming from the wrong direction, transport should be arranged for the dog/handler teams if they must travel rather long distances to an appropriate starting point. If there is no way to transport the teams, they may be required to walk the distance and then begin their systematic sweeps. This walk often can be used to perform a hasty search along a natural or man-made terrain feature.

WIDTH OF SWEEPS

As they begin working their sectors, handlers will judge the sweep widths based on the density of vegetation and wind velocity (that nice breeze in base camp may be nonexistent in the woods). The width of sweeps may vary throughout the sector due to different levels of vegetation, terrain features and wind speed variability. However, the basic plan devised at base, once begun, must be adhered to regardless of changing conditions. If the handlers feel the conditions have changed so much as to be detrimental to thorough coverage of certain portions of the search area, those portions may need to be rechecked later in the search. Because of possible changing conditions, many handlers carry flagging tape to mark areas they have covered, or areas where minor alerts were noted that the handler feels should be rechecked under better wind conditions. Some handlers carry two different colors of tape: one for marking covered areas and one for marking alerts.

When working their sectors, handlers must pay close attention to numerous details: the dog's body language and working attitude; the map and compass; terrain features, which may or may not be marked on the map; wind direction and velocity; radio traffic; clue and track awareness; and hazards, which may range from cliffs to poisonous snakes. Handlers should not attempt any night work until they have thoroughly mastered these skills during daylight training sessions.

Handler training should include "man tracking" so that handlers are always clue conscious, even when working at night. A flashlight can often illuminate a track as well as, if not better than, sunlight. As the handlers conduct their hasty or sector searches, they should always be alert for any sign that someone has been through the area.

ONE GOOD PLAN

Handlers must always remember that the crux of a good search is a *good plan.* Following the dog on every minor alert is an excellent way to destroy the basic plan and end up with incomplete coverage. Handlers who observe alerts should stop to see how far the dog goes. If he only moves a relatively short distance before losing the scent, he may have encountered either scent residue, perhaps left by previous searchers, or scent drifting in from a distance.

In either case, continuing the planned search pattern will move the dog closer to any potential scent source. If, on the other hand, the alert is strong and continued so that the dog begins to leave the handler's sight, the handler should also move in that direction, making sure that they can return to the point where the sweep was interrupted. If the alert fails to produce a find, the dog and handler can return to the marked point and resume their search pattern.

As noted earlier, during training sessions handlers should practice drawing their route on a map as they work the sector. This will help them learn to observe terrain features and be "generally aware of their location at all times," as required in the ARDA standards. This skill is critical, since it provides the data for the probability of detection and percentage of coverage within each sector on a search. Handlers must be able to tell the operational leader how thoroughly they covered their area ("I will assign an 85-percent coverage of my sector since there was a good, steady breeze and very little dense vegetation") and the probability of detection ("Because of the good wind and terrain conditions, I think there was a 90-percent chance my dog would have found the person").

AVOIDING THE SUPERDOG SYNDROME

Not all sectors on the same search can give the same percentages. Dense swamps or woods may have a very low detection and coverage rate, and those areas may have to be rechecked. Handlers must avoid the "superdog syndrome"; in other words, do not assign high coverage and detection percentages on the assumption it makes your unit look good. Leave a little room in case one dog was not really working to his usual standards or a handler made a mapping error. No unit is ever 100-percent sure, even under the best of conditions.

Upon completion of their sectors, handlers must be prepared to explain why they worked their area in a particular way. There will be some occasions that demand ingenuity or deviation from the usual crosswind pattern. One example is a steep slope. If the wind is moving up- or downslope, it can be worked in the usual way by going back and forth across the slope. If, however, the wind is coming from one side, the handler may elect to still work back and forth on the contours, since it is far less tiring than repeatedly climbing up and down. Working into the wind in such cases reduces the detection probability since, on half of the sweeps, the wind will

Dogs must learn to work in dense brush. *Sherri Gallagher*

The search area may be quite vast. *Penny Sullivan*

be angling from behind the dog/handler team. Either the sweeps can be greatly narrowed to allow more thorough coverage or the search can be treated as a hasty search, with the lesser probability of success that implies. Handlers must be prepared to make such adjustments and decisions when planning their search.

The Hasty Search

The hasty search is intended to provide a rapid—though cursory—check of the overall search area. It serves several purposes:

- To assess terrain prior to a more thorough sector search.

- To quickly check areas of high probability, such as drainages or paths that may have "funneled" the victim.

- To provide an immediate search technique if handlers have driven a long distance and/or arrived after dark, when a sector search lasting several hours might be counterproductive.

Hasty searches can be run along trails and drainages, with the handler making occasional loops into the woods (following game trails branching off an old road provides one effective way to increase coverage). They can also be conducted along power lines or even around old buildings to check quickly for a small child who may be hiding. Sectors assigned for the next day can be given initial coverage at night by working perimeter boundaries and/or making one or two wide sweeps through the area. It is advisable for handlers to flag trails, etc., with surveyor's ribbon to mark those areas that have been covered.

While hasty searches are frequently conducted at night, one or two handlers may be assigned to perform such a search within minutes of arriving on scene during the day, as the balance of the unit prepares for full field deployment.

This technique, as with sectors, must be practiced by handlers because wind conditions are not always perfect. A trail may have to be worked into the wind or eddying may create problems for the dog in following scent to its source. In such cases, it must be remembered that a hasty is exactly what its name implies—a quick search that does not necessarily guarantee success. However, the number of people found by this method has shown it to be highly effective for the amount of time expended.

To prepare for hasty searching, handlers should practice running trails, power lines, etc. The dog should show a willingness to leave the beaten path when he picks up a scent; at times, the dog may be required to follow a track where the victim has crossed the path rather than following the air scent.

The value of practice in all types of terrain and weather will be proven on actual searches where handlers must make critical assessments of the best approach to their sectors. The unit as a whole should strive for an overall coverage of 85 percent, including both hasty searches and sectors. To achieve this will require hours of practice in thorough coverage of a large area, with all handlers recognizing the critical role they play in the unit's success.

Radio Communication

During search training, both the handlers and base operators should practice radio communications. After approximately one hour, base camp should begin a systematic radio check with all handlers to determine their location within each sector. Handlers must be prepared to respond with close grid locations and base personnel must mark those locations on the map.

Any communications initiated by the handlers must be concise and pertinent. In general, the best rule is silence unless you have extremely important information.

Communications may include:

- Reporting a clue.

- Requesting to meet another handler for consultation on boundaries.

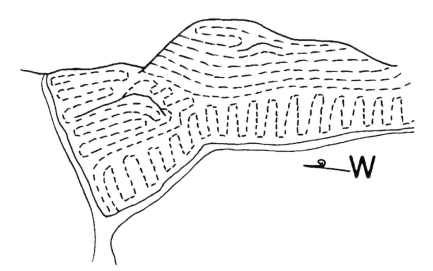

Example of varying search patterns to accommodate changes in terrain and still make use of wind currents. *Linda Warshaw*

- Reporting alerts, including those that seem to originate in an adjoining sector. (Handlers *do not* blindly charge into another handler's sector without first clearing it with the operational leader, base *and* the other handler.)

- Reporting an injury or illness of the dog or handler.

- Requesting transport back to base after completion of the sector.

- Finding the missing person.

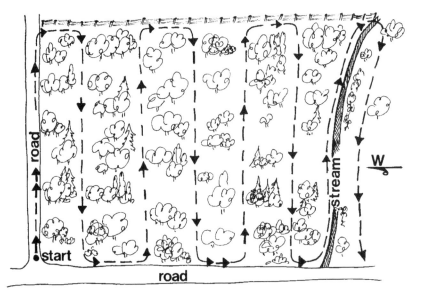

Typical crosswind sector pattern, starting on downwind side (sweeps will vary, but are normally 100 to 300 feet apart). *Linda Warshaw*

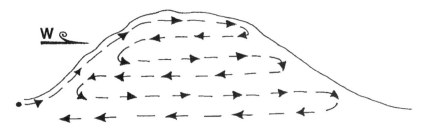

Work horizontally across a steep slope across rather than vertically up and down. *Linda Warshaw*

Varying the Search Problems

Training sessions should include, at various times, victims who are lying prone, sitting, walking, standing still, up in a tree, buried under leaves and brush, etc. The dogs must learn to find people in a wide variety of positions and situations.

The length of each problem will depend upon the training level of the team. Eventually, an operational dog should be expected to work problems lasting several hours.

One method of extending problems for each dog and at the same time practicing multiple-victim finds (so the dogs will not stop after finding one person, since actual searches often result in unexpected finds of people who are not lost) is the *round robin technique*. For example, there may be four victims hidden, one in each of four sectors. Each dog team starts with their assigned sector and, after finding the victim, moves to the next free sector and searches for that victim. Persons willing to play the role of the victim should understand that they may be in the woods for several hours, and they must be prepared to make themselves comfortable (most take along food, drink and even books).

On occasion, articles should be dropped within each sector. This serves several purposes. The dog learns to indicate a clue with human scent, while the handler can practice watching the dog closely for what may be a minor indication (since the article has less scent than the victim). In addition, it provides a motivational opportunity for the handler to play with the dog, particularly if the problem lasts several hours.

Night searching must also be scheduled regularly, since it is not at all unusual for units to receive at least half of their calls late enough to require working at night.

Additional Training

Classroom instruction should be given in scent theory, survival, map and compass, unit procedures, wilderness evacuation and search management. All these will, of course, be practiced in the field, but the basics should be taught in a classroom atmosphere where questions can be asked and suggestions considered. Experts in other fields, such as veterinarians or disaster heavy rescue specialists (people who specialize in extracating victims from beneath heavy debris), may also be brought in to lecture.

Representatives from other search organizations or official agencies may be invited to either lecture or attend your training sessions. You must learn the search structure within your state—who is in charge of what—and then, long before a search ever occurs, establish a rapport with those who will request your services. Any unit that fails to do this may not get calls.

KNOW WHEN YOU'RE WANTED

ARDA units only respond *when requested* by an official agency, because to do otherwise appears unprofessional. Should you invite yourself in, an agency may agree to let you come after you call, but you will probably be met with a reluctant welcome. On the other hand, if you respond at *their* request, you will be there because they *want* you and the atmosphere will be much more cooperative. Do your meeting and greeting before an agency actually needs you and leave the decision to them.

Base Camp

The unit's base camp is far more than a place to eat and a communications center. It becomes the hub of your search and serves as the operation's eyes and ears while handlers are in the field. Good base camp operators (BCOs) are critical to a unit's success; poor ones can destroy a unit's reputation. As stated earlier, unit workouts should always include practicing some or all aspects of base operations.

All unit members must be sufficiently skilled in running base camp to enable them to substitute or assist when necessary. Handlers whose dogs are temporarily sidelined by illness or injury and trainees whose dogs are not yet operational should be prepared to work in base.

What should BCOs prepare for? Virtually everything. A breakdown of their duties will explain why they must be highly trained in a multitude of skills.

Often, the only continuous exposure an agency has to a unit's operation is through observation of the base camp. Agencies follow strict radio procedures and they will expect the same from a volunteer unit.

RADIO COMMUNICATIONS

The BCOs should control all the unit's radio traffic. It may be advisable for handlers who wish to communicate with one another to first clear it with base to ensure that they do not interfere with other transmissions they might not be receiving on their own radio. Transmissions must be succinct, as nothing can make a unit appear more amateurish than constant chatter on the radio. The BCOs are responsible for ensuring the unit uses proper radio codes and adheres to all Federal Communications Commission regulations (including appropriate use of a call sign). All transmissions must be noted on an accurate radio log.

Additionally, the BCOs are responsible for radio security, so that unauthorized persons do not overhear transmissions. They must also be prepared to relay pertinent information and/or decisions to the OL. Unit codes must be used, since base security does not prevent those with citizen band radio base stations or police scanners from overhearing your conversations.

MAP AND COMPASS SKILLS

The BCOs must be as well-trained in map and compass skills as the handlers. They must be able to describe the sectors and search plan, and determine a given handler's location within a sector. They will be responsible for advising evacuation personnel of the handler's location when the victim is found, and the best route to that site.

SEARCH MANAGEMENT TRAINING

If the operational leader is temporarily out of contact and the agency has questions about the search plan or seeks suggestions for use of other resources, the BCO must be prepared to answer. A knowledge of subject behavior, terrain analysis and resource management is required for these situations. The agency may regard your unit as the experts and the BCOs must be prepared to provide such assistance with confidence. It is advisable for the operational leader to leave information on potential future search areas with the BCOs so that they can automatically assign those either to handlers who have finished their first assignment or to other resources.

PUBLIC RELATIONS

The one thing BCOs cannot afford is arrogance. Because of their continuous presence, the BCOs most represent the attitude of your entire unit. They must be friendly yet professional and businesslike with the agency, sympathetic and understanding with the subject's family and friends and pleasant without being too talkative to the press. They cannot give the family false hope, nor can they be too discouraging. They can give the media general information about the dog unit (how the dogs and handlers are trained, etc.), but they must refer specific questions about the search to the agency. In short, BCOs must be blessed with diplomacy and tact.

LOGISTICS

The BCOs are responsible for selecting the appropriate campsite based on traffic flow and proximity to the agency's command post. Setting up a full base operation for both local and remote situations must be practiced during unit workouts to prepare for actual missions and to test equipment. All unit personnel must be prepared to help set up the base antenna, tarp, radio, tents and cooking equipment.

The BCOs are also responsible for overseeing the well-being of the unit. They must ensure that food and drink, appropriate to the climate and working conditions, are available and they must make sleeping arrangements, if needed. They must see that sanitation rules are followed and that the base area is cleaned before the unit departs.

FIRST AID

The BCOs must meet the same standards as the handlers and be prepared to handle emergencies in base camp. They will have to coordinate any medical evacuation, including advising local personnel what extra medical supplies should be taken along. They must be aware of the needs of handlers—both in nutrition and equipment—who will spend hours working under extreme conditions. They must maintain and know how to use both the human and dog first-aid kits maintained in base camp.

The job of base camp operator is one of the most difficult in the unit and frequently requires two people. A unit cannot perform at its professional best without good BCOs.

Base camp serves as a briefing, communications and dining center for the unit. *Bill Syrotuck*

Recommended Base Camp Equipment

You will need the following items in base camp:

- **Tenting:** A four- or six-person tent can house several dog/handler teams or serve as the communications center.

- **Food:** The base camp must stock at least a five-day supply of freeze-dried meals for handlers; nutritious, high-energy snacks; coffee, tea and cold drinks; as well as a five-day supply of dog food (handlers should provide this to be stored at base, since the dogs may have different dietary requirements). It must also provide cooking equipment, including stoves, fuel, utensils, plates, cups, garbage bags and collapsible water containers (a water purification system or tablets should be included).

- **First Aid:** An extensive first-aid kit should be maintained at the base. It should include bandages, dressings, cravats, air and/or board splints, antibiotic medications, antivenom and insect sting medications, a low-reading thermometer, scissors, tweezers and, if possible, a Stokes or similar litter for medical evacuations. A separate dog first-aid kit should also be kept in base.

- **Radios:** These include the base radio, base antenna, hand-held units with at least one spare, battery chargers, extra batteries, voltmeters, spare antenna for the hand-held units and a radio repair kit (small tools, screws, nuts, bolts, etc.).

- **Documents and miscellaneous supplies:** These should include blank forms (interview sheets, radio logs); pens, pencils, markers; plastic sheeting for maps; tracing, writing and drawing paper; grids, protractors and rulers; paper clips and staples; compasses; clipboard; map board for use by the BCO; a list of emergency contact numbers for unit personnel; flashlights and batteries; unit brochures/handout sheets (useful to give the agency and the news media). Other equipment may include hatchets, hammers, small shovels, camp lights, etc.

The well-planned, well-organized base camp operation will give your unit an air of professionalism and ensure that your mission runs more smoothly. Do not be so anxious to train dogs that you overlook or shortchange this extremely important facet of search and rescue.

A TYPICAL TRAINING SESSION MAY BE AS FOLLOWS:

9:00 A.M. to Noon: Advanced dog/handler teams work sectors and/or undergo evaluation tests. Each dog may find a victim, or the workout may be a mock search with only one victim placed. Trainees can assist by serving as victims or observing the advanced teams work their sectors.

Noon to 1:00 P.M.: Entire unit practices setting up base camp; new members are expected to help so they learn the various duties. Lunch is served using unit cooking equipment.

1:00 to 2:00 P.M.: New handlers work a basic orienteering course.

2:00 to 4:00 P.M.: New dog/handler teams do line-of-sights on handlers, or similar beginner problems. While these should be practiced at home, the training officer must ensure that new teams are proceeding properly. Many new handlers assume that their dog is ready to advance simply because she comes looking for them with such eagerness. The training officer may have to curb their desire to start the dog "looking for someone else" before she is really ready. Development of the dog's play drive, particularly with nonfamily members, should be included as part of this session.

All unit workouts should be followed by a critiquing session to help with individual or unit problems. The training officer should maintain a written record of each session and of the critique itself.

Summary

Unit workouts must accomplish the following:

- Train advanced dogs in extended working times, working in various types of terrain, locating victims in unusual positions or situations, advanced agility and obedience.

- Train advanced handlers in sector coverage, radio communications, medical evacuation, map and compass work, base operations and night searching.

- Train base operators in radio communications, maintaining written records, mapping, dealing with personnel on a search and setting up and using base equipment.

- Train new handlers in dog handling, map and compass, sector coverage, scent theory and unit operations.

- Train new dogs in searching, agility and obedience.

- Refine unit procedures to ensure teamwork and thorough coverage.

- Train unit specialists, such as the operational leader, medical officer and communications officer, through mock searches, simulated medical evacuations, etc.

- Introduce the unit to outside groups and agencies involved in different aspects of search and rescue.

The operational leader is the only unit member who confers with agency representatives.
Courtesy National Park Service

10

Responding to a Search

You now feel that your dog and handler teams are competent and operationally ready. You are prepared to take on actual search missions. But before accepting any missions, your coordination system must be well-established so that the initial search call is handled rapidly—and smoothly.

Call-Out and Response

During call-out, your operational leader (OL) determines the number of handlers responding to the call and the commitment time for each (the whole unit should plan on a three-day commitment, on average). The OL then advises the agency how many members will arrive for the search and how long the dogs are available.

Once your unit responds, a rendezvous time and place should be set up. Assuming that all personnel are in a state of readiness, they should be on their way within one hour of call-out. A rendezvous is necessary to guarantee that the unit arrives as a structured, professional organization whose members immediately assume their previously assigned tasks. On rare occasions, an OL may instruct one or more *experienced* handlers who live near the search site to proceed ahead of the unit, conduct the initial interviews and perhaps run hasty searches near the point where the victim was last seen.

The agency should be given an approximate arrival time based on the driving distance between the rendezvous point and the search site. Since there may be a considerable time lapse from the OL's initial call to your arrival at the scene, you should encourage searching with other resources until you arrive. Agencies that do not work frequently with air-scenting dogs may assume that an area needs to be kept clear—agencies are often given these instructions when tracking dogs are used. A brief explanation of how air-scenting dogs work will help the agency understand that it isn't necessary to immediately suspend all other search efforts.

Once the unit arrives at the search scene, the OL should locate the agency representative to ascertain the current situation. Base personnel can then select the best location to set up base camp.

Setting Up Base Camp

The agency may already have set up their command post. BCOs should then select an appropriate site using what space is available. This site should be close to the agency's command center in order to maintain constant contact, yet it should not be in the middle of traffic flow. Dozens of people may wander through the area and you do not want them lounging around your base, distracting the BCOs and listening to potentially sensitive radio communications.

BCOs must also consider convenience factors, such as being close to dining and sanitation facilities. Space should be allotted for setting up cooking equipment. A tarp can provide a covered working or eating area.

When possible, all unit vehicles should be parked together, including the one used as base. This arrangement will enable unit handlers to leave their dogs in their cars when required and ensures that equipment is quickly available.

Other unit members can assist at base camp by setting up any external radio antenna, tarp or other equipment and checking hand-held radios to ensure that they are in good working order. Drinks and snacks will need to be prepared and made available to handlers before they enter the field. And of course, there should be ample water for all the dogs. Handlers who do not assist in setting up base should get their gear and dogs ready or help others to do so.

While unit members set up base or prepare their gear, all dogs should stay in vehicles or on leash. It isn't professional to let dogs loose so they can tear around the base camp. Also, the dogs will use up valuable energy that they need in the field.

Each unit member needs to be busy so that the group isn't rushed into the field by anxious family members who want the teams start searching right away. Obviously, you can't begin a search until you have all the pertinent information. The sight of people hard at work will deflect some of this pressure.

While working and providing a professional atmosphere, the unit should not act aloof toward the other searchers. A friendly attitude—in the midst of your preparations—is often beneficial. Information may be offered by people who have already been in the field.

Remote base setup showing separate areas for dining, sleeping, parking and command post operations.   *Linda Warshaw*

Remote search locations present an entirely different base-camp situation. The agency may have a staging area where vehicles are parked and searchers are shuttled to the command post. Under such circumstances, one unit vehicle may be allowed in the command post area to serve as the unit's headquarters, and all equipment will have to be transported in it. Even that one unit vehicle will be eliminated if the unit is flown into the search. For these reasons, the unit must have "flyaway bags" containing everything it needs to function.

Remote camps should be divided into several sections: a sleeping area, where handler tents are set up; a dining area with cooking equipment and, preferably, some type of light shelter; a base operations center with the base radio and antenna; and sanitation facilities.

Use common sense when you establish a remote base. The sanitation area should be far away from your water supply. Set up tents on a hill instead of in a drainage, where you will be extremely uncomfortable during heavy rain. Fires should be safely contained and thoroughly extinguished.

Gathering Information

Once initial contact is made with the agency representative, the OL should gather as much information as possible and should ask permission for a unit interviewer to talk to family members, friends or witnesses. Information gained from these sources is vital. To a great extent, the unit's search plan will be based on data developed from these interviews.

During the interview, certain searching information must be obtained and provided to each handler. The unit should develop an interview form upon which it can record all necessary searching data, including:

- Subject's name
- Physical description (height, weight, race, etc)
- Clothing description
- Shoe size and tread
- Discardables to watch for as clues (cigarette brand, chewing gum or candy wrappers)
- Equipment the subject may have carried (backpack, canteen, flashlight)

In addition to the searching data, the OL will need certain information critical to developing a search plan. This information must also be written on the interview form and be provided to each handler:

- Point last seen (PLS): The OL should physically inspect the PLS instead of relying on a point marked on the map (which may be incorrect). The OL should attempt to see things from the victim's viewpoint. If the missing person is a four-year-old child, the OL should get down to the approximate eye level of a small child. Is there an inviting opening in the brush that a taller person might not see? The OL should also determine the direction in which a person could disappear from sight most quickly ("I only turned my back for a minute and she was gone").
- Time last seen.
- Weather at time of loss. (For example, did the rain that raised the creek so it could not be crossed occur before or after the person was lost?)
- Subject category and/or activity when lost: child, elderly, hunter, hiker, mushroom picker, etc.
- Physical or mental condition: heart problem, diabetes, depression.
- Terrain: barriers, escape routes, etc.

The Importance of Interviews

Your unit may have one or more interviewers, depending on its size and capability. While interviewing often falls to the OL, other unit members should be able to conduct an interview if more than one witness needs to be questioned.

Because there can be a lot of available information, do not reach a conclusion before you have all the data. Conduct all interviews one-on-one, away from crowds. The last thing you want is someone constantly interrupting with, "That's not the way it happened." Other people will have a chance to present their version of events during a separate interview. It's difficult to figure out what is fact and what is fiction when you are faced with several versions of one event. You need to sort through all available data before making a judgment call.

TAKE YOUR TIME

Be considerate in all your interviews. This may be your hundredth search, but it is probably the family's first. Behave in a calm, professional manner tempered with a friendly, sympathetic attitude. Even though you may be anxious to get teams into the field, act as though you have all the time in the world. Pleasant patience can make the interview easier for both you and the person you are questioning.

Interviews provide critical data, but other factors (terrain features, for instance) also have an impact. Regardless of any other planning data, however, your interview must be thorough. A search begins with information and proceeds on the constant input of more information. You cannot get half the answers and expect to solve the entire problem. A successful search begins with successful interviews.

STRIVE TO ENSURE ACCURACY UP FRONT

Be well prepared before starting any interview. Know what information you expect to receive from each person, what information you must have to plan your search, and strive to ensure accuracy. You cannot keep repeating, "Are you *sure* she was wearing a blue blouse?"—but you will be surprised how often a person has on a different color blouse than she was described wearing.

Each person interviewed presents special opportunities and problems.

Family Members

Family members are under tremendous stress, whether they show it or not. Some people may seem very calm, while others will act quite agitated. Because interviewing is an ongoing process, your interviewer should be prepared to handle a wide range of emotions during the course of a search.

Friends

If friends were the last ones to see the missing person—particularly if the

The operational leader must plan the search based on data from interviews, victim behavior statistics and terrain analyses. *Tony Novack*

A rushing stream may present an obvious barrier that would stop or "funnel" the lost person.
Bill Syrotuck

disappearance occurred during a group outing—be *sure* to interview each friend separately. They might have worked out a story among themselves, and individual interviews may bring out inconsistencies in their story. When conducting these interviews, do not assume that there was any wrongdoing in their activity—they may simply be afraid that they will be blamed for the incident.

Witnesses

The value of a witness depends on many factors. Did they know the person, or did they simply see someone who matched the person's description? Be cautious of information from witnesses who claim to have seen the person after the subject was reported missing, particularly if they do not actually know the person. False leads can result in wild-goose chases to areas far from the primary search site. You don't want to spread resources so thin that they lose their effectiveness. While these sightings should not be immediately dismissed, neither should they be allowed to instantly alter your original search plan. Continue your coverage until you have something concrete or suggest the use of other resources to follow up on such leads.

Agency Personnel

Agency personnel can include law enforcement officers (including park rangers), rescue squads, fire departments, etc.

Law enforcement officers generally have primary responsibility for the search and are usually extremely knowledgeable. If they have been on their job for many years or were raised in the area, this knowledge is invaluable. They will frequently know whether the person has a history of mental or physical problems, if there is trouble within the family or if the episode is totally out of character. They will also have access to unusual information that you may need, such as the local weather at the time of loss or the effects of a particular medication, through contacts at the county hospital.

Law enforcement personnel are usually extremely cooperative because they asked for your help. It is rare for an agency to withhold critical information from a unit whose assistance they specifically requested.

Rescue squad and fire department personnel can also be extremely helpful. If they have looked for the person before, they will be more than happy to tell you where they found him the last time and where they think he might be this time. Like law enforcement officers, they live in the community and have a very effective grapevine. Much of the input from this group will be gathered over a cup of coffee rather than through a formal interview. An astute base operator can glean this information during casual conversation. Always bear in mind that some of these people—many of whom are volunteers themselves—may feel resentment when outsiders are brought in to do what they consider to be *their* job. Always respect their opinions and suggestions.

Maps

Having a topographical map available on every search isn't easy. Your unit should consider purchasing maps for your local search area through the U.S. Geological Survey so that you will have an original and copies immediately available upon call-out.

If you do not have unit-provided maps, you will have to rely on the agency to obtain the necessary maps (including copies for the handlers). You should state this need during the first telephone contact, before the unit's departure for the search. If an agency is unsure where to obtain topo maps, you might suggest the county zoning office or a similar local agency that uses maps for surveys, etc. In cases where the agency cannot provide a topo map, you may have to rely on a less satisfactory aerial photographic or a county road map. Handlers will have to use all their mapping skills to be effective when using these maps.

When you work from an agency-provided map, check in the lower right corner for the date when it was last photo-revised. Some old maps won't show recent developments or new roads. Older maps are still useful, but you should be aware of possible changes that could affect your search plan. Local people familiar with the area can usually tell you where the changes are; these should be marked on both your base map overlay and on the handlers' maps.

A handler reviews her assignment with the operational leader. *Gamble McCown*

11

Conducting the Search

Once all available information is collected, your Operational Leader will plan the search strategy. Any plan must be approved by the agency. You must never overlook the fact that the agency has ultimate control—and responsibility—for the search. Some agencies may, however, relinquish control to the unit and not interfere with your decisions. Others may insist that you search certain areas even though you feel those areas have a low probability. In either case, it is the agency's decision. If you must search what you consider unlikely areas, do so without complaining. If you respond to agency requests with courtesy and a positive attitude, they are far more likely to invite your suggestions during the search.

Planning the Search

The OL should study all terrain features on the map that may affect the victim's travel route. Are there major barriers that would either be impassable or so obvious that the person would follow them (major roads, lakes, cliffs)? What about minor barriers that can be crossed (small roads, an old fence, a small creek)? Are there any "confusion factors," such as obliterated trail markers or subtle terrain changes? Is there anything that might funnel the victim in one direction, such as

The Operational Leader briefs unit members before teams enter the field. *Tony Campion*

Dogs from a Maine search unit wait patiently while their handlers study a map of the search area. *Sally Thibault*

a drainage or connecting clearings? Is there anything that would trap the person, such as an area with a funneling drainage with sides that become progressively steeper and end in a sheer wall?

As you assess each of these possibilities, keep in mind victim behavior statistics. If there are three drainages, which fits the median distance traveled by a person in this victim's category? If most victims in this category are found downhill (people rarely turn around to go back uphill once they have started down), which slope best lends itself to the category statistics?

All unit members must attend a briefing to discuss the proposed search. During this briefing, they will be given information gathered to this point. Handlers should have maps of their areas or be prepared to draw them from the base camp map. The agency may be present for part of the unit briefing to provide information and input into the planning process, as well as answer any questions.

Based on all the information gathered, the OL will select prime areas to be searched and present them during the briefing. When assigning dog/handler teams, the OL must consider the strengths and weaknesses of each to ensure that the less-experienced teams are given sectors they can easily handle. If handlers express keen interest in a particular area, they should be allowed to search that area. The OL may also make a decision about the type of immediate search to be conducted—hasty searches or sector assignments. While both may be used at the same time, existing conditions often dictate which is most appropriate.

Beginning the Search

Ideally, the unit should start searching within one hour of arriving on the scene (although one or two handlers may be instructed to begin hasty searches much earlier). All interviews, planning and unit organization should be completed within that time frame.

SECTOR SEARCHES

If you arrive early in the day and handlers are well rested, you may begin with sector assignments. If, however, it is night and the unit has driven several hours, a hasty search of potential escape or funneling routes may be the best approach. Any area hastily searched at night must be included in sector search plans for daylight.

HASTY SEARCHING

The nighttime hasty search is an initial terrain evaluation, which provides important planning data. Each handler must give a detailed report on the features they find during a hasty. An area that seemed to have high potential on the map may be placed in a lower priority because the handler reports that it is full of thick, impassable briers. Old trails not shown on the map may be discovered, marked on the handler's map for future reference, and quickly searched. Hasty searches of an

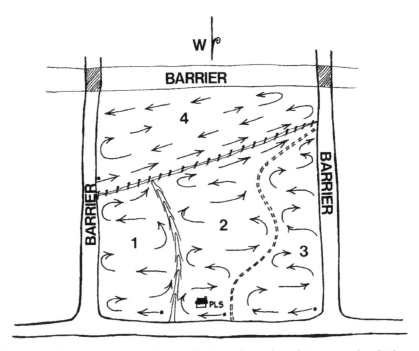

Primary search area as determined by major barriers; obvious boundaries are used to divide the area into sectors. *Linda Warshaw*

Hasty search techniques, with handlers working escape or funneling routes (trail, drainage and power line). *Linda Warshaw*

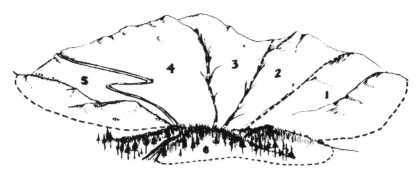

Large search area divided into sectors. *Jean Syrotuck Whittle*

area's periphery can prove particularly useful to a handler in initially surveying an area scheduled to be searched more thoroughly at daylight.

NIGHT SEARCHING

Night searches (by hasty and/or sector searches) *should* be conducted whenever possible. Victims are far less likely to move in the dark (if they doze, it is unlikely that they will sleep; therefore, victims may respond to someone who calls their name). Additionally, cooler evening air produces better scenting conditions, making dogs one of the most effective tools for night searches. Remember that a victim's chance of survival may decline rapidly—time is of the essence.

Care of Returning Teams

When handlers return to base, they will be debriefed individually by the OL. They must mark their route through assigned areas on the base map overlay and should give their coverage estimation. Handlers should detail all major terrain features, particularly if they change an area's priority. All data received from the returning handlers will be compiled and added to the overall strategy.

Base camp personnel should have food and drink available when handlers return from the field and ensure any overnight lodging arrangements have been made. Units must be adaptable—they may be housed in a nice motel or the county jail. Remote search locations rarely offer luxury accommodations—unit members must be ready to pitch their tents.

Before suspending the search for the night, a group debriefing should be held to develop a preliminary search plan for the next day based on handler input. Base camp personnel must ensure that any additional information they have developed is included in this debriefing. As with the earlier briefing, the agency may be present; however, any information handlers have that is speculative can be aired later, when only unit members are present. The agency must be advised on the overall search plan, but some situations call for discussions restricted to the unit.

Continuing the Search

Hold a unit briefing on each full day of searching before teams enter the field. This briefing must provide handlers with newly developed information and explain the day's overall search plan. Each team must have a map and be absolutely certain of sector boundaries.

Handlers should enter the field as soon as the preliminary briefing ends. Because they will depend on their radios for hours, a radio check between each handler and base should be done before the handler leaves.

Someone may need to accompany handlers if a sector is extremely rugged. Unit trainees can and should be used for this purpose as the experience they gain will be invaluable when they are operational. Give serious consideration to well-equipped, competent family members or friends of the victim who want to go with the handlers. It may be better for them to accompany trained searchers instead of wandering around on their own.

Training on different vehicles pays off as a dog team prepares for transport to their sector on a snowcat. *Jeff Doran*

USING VOLUNTEERS

When the agency is present at the unit briefing, the OL may be asked which areas not being covered by dogs can be searched by local volunteers. The agency may face 100 impatient people who want to join the search, but it may be reluctant to commit these volunteers for fear of interfering with the dogs. The OL should help determine how to best use these resources.

A search dog may find himself transported in unusual ways. This dog prefers a window seat. *Penny Sullivan*

Open areas with good visibility can be grid-searched by volunteers, while the dog teams should check areas where a dog's scenting ability may be the only way to locate a victim. Four-wheel drive groups can run logging roads and transport searchers. There are numerous ways to use local volunteers without interfering with the dogs. Both the agency and the volunteers will appreciate a "we're all in this together" attitude. Another benefit of using volunteers is an increased Probability of Detection (POD) with each search of a given area.

STATIONARY LOOKOUTS

Some volunteers can be strategically posted as stationary lookouts along roads, power lines and other potential escape routes. If these volunteers can see a fairly long distance in either direction, they will be ideally placed to spot a victim who wanders out of the woods. Other volunteers can drive cars along perimeter roads and serve the same purpose on a moving basis. Both uses contain the search area so that the victim is seen and stopped before he goes any farther and gets into more trouble.

KEEP IN MIND

Remember the following things:

- Locals familiar with the search area can be extremely helpful and—if they offer to work with the handlers—should be allowed to.

- Law enforcement agencies may provide an officer to work with each handler. Most are willinng to follow the handler's direction and adopt the team as their own, remaining with them throughout the search.

- Handlers have ultimate responsibility for their sectors. They must ensure that people who accompany them remain close *behind* and follow their instructions.

POTENTIAL DESTINATIONS

Other volunteers can check potential destinations. Confused, elderly people who have been raised in the area may talk occasionally about "going home." This usually refers to the place where they spent their childhood. Volunteers should periodically check these locations.

Radio Transmissions and Media Interviews

A base camp operator must stay at the radio 100 percent of the time, maintaining accurate logs of each radio transmission and each handler's progress. The BCO will frequently be visited by the agency, family members, neighbors, other searchers and the media. The media must be referred to the agency for *all* information on the search. Speculation to a reporter or unwittingly revealing sensitive information is disastrous for a unit's professional reputation. If reporters ask general questions about the unit itself, the BCO can answer them, or if extremely busy, politely arrange an interview when the OL returns from the field. Family members, too, should have limited access to radio transmissions so that any bad news can be broken to them in an appropriate manner rather than hearing it over the radio.

If interference from onlookers is too great, the BCO may request help from the agency in securing the area. The BCO walks a delicate line between being totally cut off from everyone—and thereby missing an important bit of information—and being overrun. Using a properly instructed trainee as a base assistant will reduce some of these problems.

Clues

A clue can be a piece of clothing, a candy wrapper or a footprint. Untrained searchers often overreact when they find clues. Searchers can send an anxious family on an emotional roller coaster if they excitedly proclaim they have found a clue before its connection to the subject can be proven.

Searchers should be subdued and cautious when they report any clues. Keep all information between the unit and the agency until you determine its validity. Use a special code to radio discovery of a clue in order to avoid raising false hopes among bystanders.

Flag all clues and leave them as you found them, unless the agency authorizes their removal. The BCO must immediately mark the location of a clue on the base map. If the clue is *positively* identified as belonging to the victim, the clue and its location will become the new "point last seen," since it is obvious that the person was in the area. This will in all probability have a major impact on your search plan.

The Unit Find

Whether you are on your first search or your 50th, there is no sense of accomplishment quite like a unit find. When a dog performs exactly as he does in training—with a strong alert, close-in, recall/refind—handlers will understand why so many hours of work were necessary. The entire unit will share the handler's feeling of pride, no matter which dog makes the find.

Handlers must be prepared to cope with any situation involving the victim. If a person is alive and well, evacuation may include nothing more than leading the individual back to base. If the person is ill or injured, the handler will need to use his first-aid and evacuation skills. In either case, handlers may require assistance from base camp. A physically well person may manifest emotional problems— either from the trauma of being lost or from problems that led him to become "lost" in the first place (such as depression, possibly to the extent of being suicidal). In such cases, the handler may have to coax the person into returning home or may request that the base send a family member, an agency representative or someone else who the person trusts.

Handlers should assume that evidence may be in an area around a find, and avoid disturbing the immediate vicinity. *Penny Sullivan*

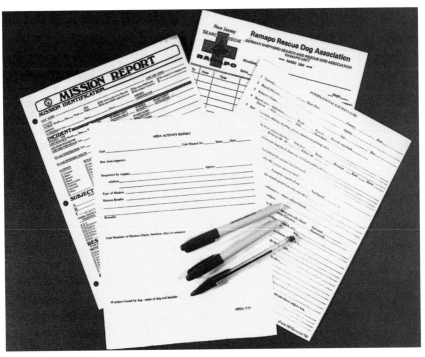

Document all searches including interviews, mission reports and radio logs. *Peggy Williams*

Looking for Evidence

If the victim is deceased, the handler should assume there is evidence in the area that will help determine the cause of death. In the case of an obviously violent death, it is essential to preserve the scene as foul play may be involved. The handler should reward his dog far enough away from the scene so that he doesn't disturb any evidence in the vicinity.

Handlers need to be mentally prepared to deal with deceased subjects. Their dog's actions will give advance notice that someone is in the vicinity and the handler should emotionally prepare to find a body.

When making a find, the handler will radio the grid coordinates and subject's condition to the base, along with any request for assistance. Base will record the coordinates on the map and the exact time on the radio log. If foul play is involved, the agency may require this information for a criminal trial. The handler will also note everything about the scene and be prepared to describe the dog's performance, since handlers are sometimes required to testify as witnesses during a trial.

ARDA has a general policy of not revealing to the news media the names of the dog and handler making the find. This policy is based on the knowledge that any operational team is capable of making the find and it is a matter of chance which handler was assigned to the correct area. All finds are considered a successful unit effort, not the sole accomplishment of one dog or handler.

Suspending the Mission

Obviously, a successful mission ends when the missing person is found. On many occasions, however, your unit will need to suspend a mission without finding the subject. This is never easy, but circumstances often dictate when you will have to head home, including:

- All logical areas have been searched. If you have spent three days on the scene and thoroughly searched several square miles, there may simply be no logical place left to cover. This must be a joint decision with the agency, or the agency may independently decide to end the effort.

- New information is received indicating the subject has left the area. As with a clue, suspending the search must be based on fact rather than rumor. Again, the agency will make the final decision, depending upon their assessment of the information's reliability.

- Unit members must return home or go to work. The commitment time should have been explained to the agency when the unit was first contacted. Most agencies understand that members have other responsibilities. If some members can stay for an extra day or two, the agency may welcome their presence. If the OL must leave, suggestions for new search areas should be left with the agency and the handlers.

If you must suspend your efforts even though the subject has not been found, it is a relatively frequent practice for units to offer to train in the area on weekends, if the search site is not too far from home. Such training must be conducted with the agency's permission for reasons of professional courtesy and legalities (to avoid problems with trespassing, for instance).

Documentation

You will need to document all aspects of each mission. Documents provide written records in case legal questions are raised about the conduct of the search. Documents also enable you to accurately critique your mission.

Documentation should include:

- Radio logs that show the nature of each transmission with the handler's unit number, the time and grid coordinates.

- Interview sheets.

■ Maps that show the handlers' routes through their sectors, the boundaries of each sector, probabilities of detection, where there were alerts, and where clues and/or the subject was found.

■ A mission report form that includes weather (temperature and conditions, such as rain or snow), wind direction and velocity, type(s) of terrain, the name of the requesting agency with a contact number and individual, subject category and how the mission was concluded (if the subject was found, by whom and how far from the PLS). You may want to include a list of other resources the agency used, such as mounted searchers, helicopters, grid searchers, etc. The report should also show the names of unit members who responded and how many days they were on the search.

Maintain a separate folder on each mission for ready reference. This complete documentation will help your study of victim behavior and the effects of weather, wind and terrain on your dog's scenting ability.

Introduce dogs to divers before training starts so that the diver's unusual appearance—in mask and wetsuit—won't startle the animal. *Bob Snyder*

12

Special
Applications

*Once you train your dog for air scenting, she can be used on
a wide variety of difficult searches. This chapter includes
training techniques for some of the more unusual missions
where your assistance may be requested.*

Water Search Training

Before handlers start water training, they should understand currents, tides, deposition zones, thermoclines (layers of water between warmer surface zones and colder, deeper zones where the temperature decreases rapidly with depth), underwater contours and depths and their resulting effect on scent.

The best place to begin water training is in a privately owned pond or the private part of a lake where there are no bystanders or nearby neighbors who will create conflicting scent. If there are people in the area, be sure that they remain downwind of the working area (this also applies on actual searches).

Although some work will be done in shallow water near the shore, the ideal water depth is generally 10 to 12 feet. This minimizes surface disturbance and maximizes good scent flow. All training should be done with divers to ensure a reliable source of human scent.

You will need a diver who is thoroughly briefed on how the dogs work—both from a boat and from shore. The diver will advise you of the best way to give a "surface" signal, as you want the diver to surface as soon after the alert as possible to quickly reinforce the dog. Divers may or may not wear wetsuits. The dogs will be able to detect them either way.

AVOIDING SURFACE DISTURBANCES

Perhaps of most concern to handlers is the diver's air tank, which will periodically emit bubbles and might give away the diver's location. Because divers often have no choice but to use these tanks, handlers must avoid inadvertently training their dogs to respond to this visual cue and instead encourage them to react only to the airborne scent.

Divers relatively close to the surface emit large, intermittent bubbles in concert with their breathing, which increases the possibility of inadvertently cueing the dog. However, the pressure in deeper water affects the diver's exhaled air by causing rising bubbles to expand until they break into smaller bubbles that create far less surface disturbance. Obviously, the deeper the diver, the less distracting the bubbles. If a diver is in very shallow water, a snorkel may be a solution to this problem.

For an initial introduction to water detection, it is advisable to start each dog with the runaway game. Allow the dog to watch the diver enter the water. (Owners can work very young dogs by themselves, wading into the water and hiding behind reeds or lying in the water if it is warm enough.)

A gradual offshore slope is ideal for this training, so that your dog does not have to swim to reach the diver. While all search dogs must know how to swim,

Dog alerts toward diver during a shore problem. *Bob Snyder*

During more advanced training, dogs are allowed to watch divers leave for deeper water.
Penny Sullivan

the purpose of this session is a quick, easy find. The diver should carry a ball or stick, showing it to the dog as an enticement just before wading into the water. The dog can then be released on the Find command and allowed to race out to the diver. The ensuing play session can be carried out onshore to ensure the dog receives a strong, prolonged reward.

Advanced dogs with actual search experience often don't need this introduction—they will react to human scent regardless of its source. For intermediate dogs who are given runaway problems, once or twice should be enough. These dogs should be nearly mission-ready and quickly understand what is expected of them.

When searching from a boat, the dog should display an alert, working attitude. *Courtesy of Gamble McCown*

Dog alerts on diver by dipping her nose to the water. *Peter Bremy*

If a dog does not respond eagerly, don't attempt advanced work until she successfully completes these problems.

The next step is a shoreline search without the dog watching the diver leave. The diver should be totally submerged just offshore. Again, this shore problem enables the handler to give the dog an immediate, enthusiastic play session. This won't be possible in the confines of a boat during later advanced work. Reward sessions are critical to maintain your dog's interest. Take full advantage of the reward opportunities presented by shore problems.

Once your dog eagerly indicates the diver's location from shore, she can progress to work in the boat. When you select the boat for this training session, consider safety factors along with the dog's comfort, so that she can concentrate on the search problem. The boat should be low, close to the water, stable and maneuverable.

Diver rewards dog with stick. *Peter Bremy*

INCREASING THE DOG'S INTEREST

It is acceptable for the handler to let his dog watch as the diver swims or is taken by boat to deeper water. The diver may call to the dog or make a motion to attract her attention before he disappears under the water. The handler should verbally increase the dog's interest in the diver: "Where's he going? Look at that!" If a single boat transports the diver *and* carries the dog, it should quickly return to shore to pick up the dog while her interest is at its peak. A dog who squeaks and whines to go after the diver is exhibiting maximum motivation and must be allowed to work while her eagerness is high.

At this point, the boat operator is a critical player who must understand how wind and water currents affect the dog's ability to pick up scent. The boat operator will have to maneuver his boat accordingly. The handler must also know the diver's location at this stage and should only concentrate on the dog and observe her individual alert.

HITTING THE SCENT QUICKLY

On the first problem, the operator should put the boat directly downwind of the diver so the still-enthusiastic dog can hit the scent quickly. The dog should be sitting or standing upright in the front of the boat where she can pick up all the air currents washing over the bow. A dog who rides with her head hanging over one side of the boat may miss scent coming from the front or the other side. Such a close scan is unnecessary and—by limiting the scenting scope of the dog—may even prolong the search. The handler should be sitting behind her dog, relaxed yet encouraging. A leash may or may not be used, depending upon the conditions.

The handler will learn to read his dog here and he should pay close attention. Some dogs will bark and try to jump out of the boat; others will lean over the side of the boat and bite at the water. Some dogs simply lift their noses and keep them lifted until they lose the scent.

Once the dog alerts, the diver should surface using a prearranged signal. The diver can have the dog's ball or can take it from the handler upon surfacing and give it to the dog. As with the runaway game, this problem—with the visual cue of watching the diver leave—only needs to be practiced once or twice with an intermediate or advanced dog.

The next step is the final preparation for an actual mission. The dog will not be allowed to see the diver disappear and the handler will not know the diver's location. The boat operator, who *must* know the diver's location, will be requested to work in a grid pattern back and forth, downwind of the search area. The handler should gauge the width of the sweeps based on wind velocity and estimated detection distance. The boat operator must be in a position to advise if there are any subtle alerts that the handler misses.

This is a learning experience for both dog and handler. The boat operator will again be a critical link in making sure the dog succeeds. This entire exercise can be ruined by an operator who remains silent and continues a search pattern long after passing the diver. If a dog is taken through an area, alerts repeatedly and gets no reward because the handler fails to read her properly, she will either lose interest or decide it is the wrong scent. This same problem of losing interest will occur on real missions. The best solution is to mark the alert area after one or two sweeps and then have at least one other dog taken through the area to see if she, too, indicates scent.

REWARDING THE DOG

On a training problem, the purpose is to reinforce and reward the dog, not to see how long she stays interested in the scent. If the operator notes an alert based on prior knowledge of the diver's location but the handler misses or misreads it, the operator should advise the handler. After a few similar problems, the handler should become adept at reading his dog. This skill is the essence of success on search missions and must be developed with practice.

It is an inescapable fact that polishing the dog's performance can only be accomplished on real missions. Many drownings occur where underwater debris or currents make a training simulation impossible. Once your dog has successfully worked training problems, however, she will generally indicate human scent regardless of the circumstances. Practice should also continue with the dog working from shore since water conditions on some searches may preclude the use of a boat.

Handlers should practice problems with the dog working on divers from directions other than downwind. Bringing the dogs in from all four directions has frequently proven highly effective in more accurately pinpointing the victim's location. Pay attention to the difference between an alert on scent residue—which is often encountered in deposition zones (areas along river shorelines downstream of the subject's location)—and alerts on the subject. Residue alerts are usually much less pronounced than alerts on the subject.

The difficulties of drowning missions lie in two areas:

1. Pinpointing the source of the scent because of water or current drift.

2. Adequately rewarding the dog.

To successfully pinpoint scent, handlers must be educated in the nuances of wind, water currents and thermoclines, as well as the effect of debris and deposition zones.

Exercise care when you reward your dog for indications that can't be proven due to the difficulty of body recovery. Highly motivated dogs can survive a lack of reward on a water search if there is any doubt—just as they do on land searches when they don't make a find. Maintain your dog's enthusiasm with periodic training problems that culminate in strong reward sessions.

THE SEEK OR LOOK COMMAND

When you train for avalanche, article or forensic cadaver search, use the Seek, Look for it, Search or the German *Such* (*zookh*) command. Choose a word that feels comfortable to you and that doesn't sound like another basic command. You may decide to use a phrase rather than a single word, such as Look for it. The intent here is to indicate to your dog that you want her to use a modified form of searching.

SEARCHING FOR SUBTLE SCENT

In wilderness searches, your dog searches in response to the Find command using a wide-ranging pattern with head held high checking the wind. The scent is detectable from quite a distance, and is obviously a person once the dog closes in.

In the close work encountered with buried subjects or when a small item needs to be located, dogs must learn to look for a puddle of scent on the surface that may be detectable downwind for only very short distances. When the dog closes in on a buried or concealed person, the apparent source will *not* be obvious and the dog must learn to dig down to the true source. Once she understands that the person is *below* the surface, she will quickly learn to move her nose closer to the ground and carefully scan the surface while she keeps the ranging pattern closer, slower and more thorough.

When you train this command for avalanche work, it is important not to condition a dog to think that all snow work is avalanche work. One example is when you look for a missing hunter in late fall. While the environment is snow, you could be looking for someone perched on a stump, collapsed in the shelter of some trees or fallen in the open and covered by a foot of new snow. This victim is certainly not buried in the debris of boulders and blocks of snow, as an avalanche victim would be. In fact, this type of victim emanates a large amount of scent, even through snow cover. Consequently, while this is

This dog is performing a close, nose-to-the-ground search on the Seek or Look command. *Doug Stanley*

definitely a snow environment, the Find command would be much more efficient. Practice both wilderness and avalanche searches in the snow, using their different techniques.

RESPONDING TO THE COMMAND, NOT THE ENVIRONMENT

When your dog responds to the command and not only to her environment, you will discover that the chosen command is useful for many applications. Consider the consequence of a bomb explosion where a person was blown into small pieces. It was necessary for SARDA teams to retrieve as many of these pieces as possible for analytic examination to determine the cause of the explosion. The pieces were driven into the ground, plastered against the trees and, in many instances, were smaller than one-quarter square inch. The sixty pounds of material recovered required a thorough, nose-close-to-the-ground scanning technique. The Seek command was used, which told the dog, "I want you to thoroughly scan the surface for an extremely small intensity of scent and show me its source." (This type of forensic cadaver search is addressed more thoroughly in Chapter 14.)

If, on a wilderness search in the middle of summer, there is suspicion that a lost child was murdered and buried in a shallow grave, the Seek command can be used for scanning specific areas. The Find command would be used for general searching (perhaps the child is really just lost).

It is important that your dog isn't conditioned to think all snow work is avalanche work. *Bill Syrotuck*

Article searching can be done with the same command, but you don't need to train for this excessively. A brief article search once a month or so will maintain the dog for use on evidence searches. Although you want a dog who will indicate articles on a wilderness search, precious time can be lost on avalanche or disaster missions if your dog indicates—and digs—for every article of clothing while the victim lies nearby. A skilled handler should note and quickly check each indication by the dog, whether subtle or intense. If there is any doubt, the handler can mark the site so that digging parties can investigate further while the dog continues searching. Except in specifically designated evidence searches, your primary purpose is to find people.

SEARCHING FOR EVIDENCE

An evidence search must be slow and meticulous, inspecting every inch of surface, since the object sought is often very small or hidden. The dog may be searching for body fluids in the soil, small pieces of human tissue, articles retaining scent residue—such as gloves, shotgun shells, wallets—or the body of a buried homicide victim.

While the dog has already been trained to indicate articles when she searches for a person on the Find command, evidence search requires the slow, nose-to-the-ground work previously described in this chapter in the Seek command section (page 161). In addition, the hand signals for a directed wilderness search may be used to produce a quartering evidence search pattern, with the dog moving slowly back and forth in front of her handler.

TRAINING FOR EVIDENCE SEARCHES

Early training may be conducted by hiding your dog's favorite toy or stick—after it has been thoroughly handled to ensure some strong human scent—in an obvious location. When your dog finds the object, reward her with an enthusiastic play session. Most dogs quickly understand this new game, so you can progress to hiding different, well-scented articles (leather wallets, keys, etc.).

Some handlers encourage dogs to pick up the item, since an alert on a real mission may be so subtle that the handler overlooks the object. Others train for a passive (Sit or Down) alert. Eventually, you should be able to hide items under leaves, in a brush pile and similar places. ARDA recommends that you occasionally throw an object instead of placing it, so that there is no track for the dog to follow. Just as with multiple-victim finds in wilderness searches, dogs should learn to search for several objects.

SEARCHING CRIME SCENES

Any search can become a criminal case. For example, at an initial briefing it is known only that a person is missing, not whether a crime has been committed. A dog team then finds the missing subject, who is deceased. Unless proven otherwise, the area should be treated as a crime scene. If the handler observes that the person appeared to die an unnatural death, he should look for anything suspicious about the position of the body, a weapon near the body or any details that concern the location of the body (lying on top of the ground, in water, or covered by rocks or branches).

As the first person on the scene, the handler is responsible for protecting the area. While he waits for the authorities to arrive, the handler should not unnecessarily walk in the immediate vicinity of the body. The general rule is: "One way in, same way out." Reward and leave the dog some distance from the scene. To avoid destroying evidence, do not pick up or touch anything. Carefully observe the

SEARCHING FOR SMALL REMAINS

All crime scene searches are not necessarily for a body. Some searches only involve portions of human remains. In these cases, dogs help authorities determine that a crime has *not* occurred, such as in the following case. In the course of leveling the backyard of a new home being built over the site of a burned-out hotel, a human skull was found. Hair was still attached to this skull, indicating a possible crime. ARDA dogs searched dirt piles that had already been removed from the scene and deposited in another part of the village. The dogs found the frontal portions of two different human skulls. When searching the backyard later, the dogs alerted in a number of places. Anthropologists systematically searched the alert areas and found a complete cemetery with bones estimated to be 80 to 100 years old.

In another instance, dog teams were requested to search an area where a human skull was found the day before. Again, this indicated a possible crime scene. The medical examiner stated that a better identification could be made if the skull's three missing front teeth were found. The leaf-covered surface where the skull was discovered had been disturbed while searchers were looking for the skeleton. Two dogs searching the area alerted to a small pile of leaves, where the three teeth were found. The time of death was estimated at three years prior to the body's discovery. The Seek command was used in both of these instances.

area, making notes of what you see or may have seen during the search, and be sure to include the times that they occurred. Handlers may be required to testify later at an inquest or before a grand jury, which will not be the time to rely on memory. (Records maintained by base camp personnel may also be requested by the prosecutor or defense attorney; this makes it imperative to keep accurate radio logs and map notations).

No matter whether the subject is alive or deceased, disturb the area as little as possible when determining the subject's condition and treating any injuries. Recovering evidence is just as critical in the case of a live assault victim as it is with a homicide victim.

Above all, do not discuss the case with anyone other than law enforcement officers. The most innocent-looking individual may be responsible for the missing person's situation. What seems like idle conversation to you may actually provide the suspect with time to destroy valuable evidence. All questions that pertain to the missing subject or the search strategy must be referred to the responsible agency.

In the event that a confession by a homicide suspect is inadmissible, dog handlers who participated in the search may be required to testify as expert witnesses in relation to both training and search experience (written training logs should be maintained for this very purpose). ARDA handlers have testified as expert witnesses to the "inevitable discovery" of a double homicide when the confession was inadmissible. In that case, dog teams were working in the direction of the bodies, which were discovered by other means. The prosecutor used the "inevitable discovery" approach to require the handlers to testify that, had they continued, the dogs would have inevitably discovered the bodies.

> *When handlers are working known or possible criminal cases, they must be extremely professional in what they do and say. To be thorough, handlers must practice clue awareness and man-tracking skills (noting bits of paper, disturbed rocks and broken branches). The hopes of many people rest upon the teamwork of the dog and handler trained to provide answers to an already difficult case.*

In 1969, Jean Syrotuck's dog was the first American-trained dog to make an avalanche find.
Courtesy of National Park Service

13

Avalanche Training

Carefully select training aids when you prepare dogs for avalanche work. All training should be done with live "victims" unless you have no alternative. It's debatable whether or not you should use clothing in practice. While clothing is certainly easier (and quicker) to use than human volunteers, your ultimate goal is for your dog to find human victims. Therefore, you should direct all training toward this goal. When clothing is used in practice, dogs often see it as being as important as the victim—especially if the dog is praised equally whether he finds a glove or a buried body. On a real mission, where every minute counts, a dog trained with clothing may spend considerable time digging up a glove near the surface, only to have the victim die 50 feet away. It is no achievement to have found 15 articles of clothing and then find the victim too late.

Victim-oriented dogs will still indicate clothing on real avalanche missions; however, the indication from the dog will be vague. A good handler will recognize that there is probably something under the surface, but realize that it is of less importance than the victim. Regardless of the dog's reaction, flag the site and call a digging party before you move on.

There is some value in orienting dogs to sound. The acoustics of snow often enable a buried victim to hear diggers far better than the diggers can hear her. There have been instances of victims shouting but not being heard by searchers. However, the SAR dog can hear the buried victim quite easily. Dogs can also hear the sound emitted by a SKADI (a personal locator transmitter) and can home in on it faster than a person trying to triangulate with a second SKADI.

PRACTICE VICTIMS AND HOLES

In the early stages of the dog's training, practice victims are buried in shallow holes and are able to free themselves easily and quickly. As training progresses, the victims will be buried deeper and deeper. Practice victims should have no trouble breathing through snow (it's porous) as long as they leave enough space for air to circulate around their nose and mouth.

Being buried underneath several feet of snow can be unnerving to the uninitiated. Without some precautions and instructions (such as using graduated burial depths and times), practice victims may be recovered in a state of shock.

When it is anticipated that the practice victims will be unable to free themselves without assistance, the following recommendations are made:

1. Dig holes with a pocket at each end to enable victims to wiggle their feet and freely move their head and shoulders. The hole should be wide enough for the victims to lie with their elbows outstretched and have several inches to spare. The victims should be consulted to ensure that they do not feel the hole is too short or too narrow. The victims should *never* enter the hole if they are short of breath.

2. On entry, the victims should lie on their stomachs and get into a comfortable position, resting on their elbows and arching their backs. Place blankets over them for the dogs to tug.

Side view of a snow cave, showing the size of the hole and the victim's placement. *Bill Syrotuck*

The dog should be encouraged to dig eagerly when he locates the victim. *Bill Syrotuck*

3. Cover the victims' feet and legs first, and then cover along their back. After you shovel about one foot of snow into the hole, the victims should relax their positions to see if the snow will stay packed. Shovelers must stop while this is being done. When it is clear that the snow will stay firm, the victims should again arch their backs and press against the snow until the hole is completely filled in from above. This procedure should leave several inches of space between the victims' bodies and the snow when they relax. During this entire process, shovelers should occasionally stop to ask the victims if everything is all right. Victims should remember that sound carries *down* through snow better than it carries *up*, and that they need to yell to be heard.

4. Add snow to the hole until it blends into the surrounding texture and snow level.

5. Thoroughly criss-cross the general area with snowshoe tracks so that there is no single path leading right to the hole. An area 20 feet around the hole should be thoroughly turned over by shovel to be sure the dog doesn't cue on the change of snow texture.

6. Maintain radio contact with the victims and be sure to make frequent checks.

While getting comfortable in the hole, victims must make sure that there are no lumps, bumps or rocks underneath them. These become very irritating in short order. Being unable to do anything about them further adds to the feeling of being encased in cement. Victims should also be well insulated against the cold because they are immobile. Bring a book and a light to help pass the time. People who have not played victim before will be surprised by how light it is inside the hole, and handlers should reassure them beforehand that they are not climbing into a deep, dark dungeon.

Using screens, boards or ski poles as the hole's roof is discouraged. In the process of digging, dogs might pierce their pads or get their paws caught in screen mesh. This kind of experience will make them reluctant to dig in the future. Exercise caution when you are working a very loosely packed hole. A dog who falls into a four- or five-foot-deep hole may become very wary of them.

TIME LAPSE VERSUS DEPTH

While it may seem that the deeper the practice victims, the more difficult the problem is for the dog, time lapse can be as important as depth. A person buried in a shallow hole for 10 minutes may emit the same amount of scent as a person buried 10 feet would emit after 30 minutes. Consequently, it is not always necessary to use deep holes to create a good training problem for your dog. Shallow holes of two to three feet should not always be used, either, as a dog can frequently tell when he has stepped on the victim. In that case, he will be cued by feel instead of scent. SARDA found that having five feet of snow above the victim is sufficient for advanced dogs, *provided* the time from burial to release of the dog was short. Under these conditions, the dog's task is to differentiate between the scent intensity of those who buried the person and the person who is buried. Since the time lapse is short, the intensity of scent at the surface will be very small.

A Georgia search dog digs for a victim in soft dirt, which is ideal for training this response for both avalanche and disaster work. *Sandy Crain*

Handlers should help the dog dig as the victim may be only a foot below the surface. *Bill Syrotuck*

Having the scents of others present in an area cannot be avoided. Since this will occur in every practice session, it becomes a challenge for your dog to detect the very low intensity of the victim's scent coming up through the snow and then discriminate that scent from the others surrounding it.

Use each hole only once, since disturbed snow and surrounding scents will act as an obvious cue for the next dog.

GROUP PRACTICE SESSIONS

ARDA recommends that you dig several holes (about three per dog) in advance. A series of short, repeated successful performances is more beneficial to your dog than a single difficult one. Therefore, dig all holes in one session. The holes should cover a wide area so that one set can be used by one dog without interfering with the performance of another dog. After all the holes are dug, the victims should wait an hour or so before being placed, so that the diggers' scents can disperse. The amount of time it takes to prepare these holes will depend upon the number of people available to help. Allow enough time in your schedule to accomplish this.

Begin the session by burying victims in several adjacent holes. There should be a minimum of two diggers. After the victims are buried and the appropriate time has passed, release the dog and begin his training. After the dog successfully finds his first victim, immediately repeat the exercise on the second and third victims. If the area is large enough, a second set of victims can be buried downwind while the first dog is working. Keep in mind that the tempo of training should be quick, with a series of rapid and successful performances that are immediately rewarded.

Alerting and Dispatching

It may be ideal to station fully trained avalanche dogs at ski areas. However, the odds of an avalanche occurring at any given American ski resort are so low that it is probably more practical to use a dog unit with all-around capabilities. Your unit may need to service five or six ski areas from one central location, so handlers must be contacted—and dispatched—rapidly.

There will always be some lag time. If the ski area is 40 miles away, it may be an hour from the time of call-out until the dog arrives on the scene. Since avalanche victim survival times are short—due to possible injury, hypothermia or suffocation—other rescue attempts (such as probe lines) will be initiated before you arrive. If the person has not been found by these means, the dog will be the best asset, even though you may have to wait up to 10 minutes to allow the scent from previous searches to dissipate. There is always a chance that the victim is alive, and you must act accordingly.

A general alerting system for dog units has already been described in Chapter 8. Avalanche work requires an even faster response. Teams should be in a constant state of readiness during high avalanche hazard conditions. Liaison should be established with local military or private helicopter facilities, with handlers aware of the potential landing sites near their homes (such as a schoolyard or a parking lot free of power lines and other hazards).

A "state of readiness" means the following:

- Handlers have immediate access to the telephone; their gear is packed and ready to go.

- During working hours at their regular jobs, handlers take their dogs and equipment to work with them. If necessary, dogs can be left in the car, but obviously they should be checked occasionally.

- During nonworking hours, handlers inform the coordinator of their whereabouts and give a contact number if they leave home for any reason. If they can't provide a telephone number, the handler must check in every hour or so. Handlers should use a cell phone or a beeper or pager to remain in constant contact.

People often respond to an avalanche call via helicopter. However, only part of the unit should be transported by air. The remainder should respond by land. Prime avalanche weather is often adverse for flying and helicopters may be grounded, turned back or unable to land due to inclement weather. Teams traveling by car may require a police escort so that heavy traffic doesn't delay the teams and cause them to lose valuable time.

WORKING AN AVALANCHE MISSION

A common misconception about working avalanches is that the area needs to be totally uncontaminated or the dogs cannot work. Actually, dogs can be used even after a probe team has gone through the area, provided that at least 10 minutes is allowed for the scent to disperse. All probe teams and other assistance should be positioned downwind so the dogs can work without interference from conflicting scents.

Digging parties of at least three people should be formed and equipped with probes and shovels. These parties should be stationed downwind from the dogs, ready to rush to a point indicated by the dog and ready to start digging once the handler marks the point. Handlers should carry a number of wands or similar marking devices.

DOG INDICATIONS ON REAL AVALANCHE MISSIONS

Each dog will develop his own distinctive alerting and digging response. The handler will normally see a nose alert, followed by checking for a precise place to begin digging. The dog will then stop and poke his nose into the snow, checking for the best direction, and then begin digging with great enthusiasm and perseverance, possibly whining at the same time.

There are times when the dog will not indicate in his usual keen manner. His reactions may be somewhat vague and indefinite. He appears to hunt around more and his digging may be tentative or nonexistent. You may realize your dog has made an indication but be unable to tell whether it is the very faint scent of a victim or the strong scent of a mitt (which the dog may ignore after some investigation). Since you cannot take the chance of making an error, you should mark the spot and proceed on your search pattern, leaving the questionable area to be searched by the digging party.

AVALANCHE RESCUE SUPPLIES

Here's a list of supplies you'll need for an avalanche mission:
- Regular first aid supplies, water, food and heat packs
- Wands to mark areas already searched
- Small snow shovels for shallow digging if the dog gives a strong indication
- Short, four or six-foot probe sticks to "feel" for the victim beneath the snow—and also to punch holes into the snow, allowing any scent below to channel to the surface

Dogs expected to work avalanche missions must learn to be transported on ski lifts. *Emil Pelcak*

The handler should not be surprised if a dog indicates four or five different places in an avalanche area. This is especially true with slab avalanches, where scent may move horizontally or at angles and then leak out on the surface in several different places. The dog may give several medium to strong alerts, appear very interested and persistent but then have trouble following through with intensive digging. At this point, the handler should evaluate the geography of the snow and cracks. The most efficient approach is to move off, have the area dug through, and then bring the dog back a short time later to attempt to determine a direction.

All handlers should have radios. When working an avalanche, the handler should occasionally report on the dog's progress. If a dog becomes fatigued or is not working well, a replacement team can be summoned with a minimum of delay.

The entire mission should have a rapid tempo—work quickly and thoroughly, mark an indication, call for a digging party, move on. Every second counts. If the dog starts digging in earnest, get on your hands and knees and start digging with him. The victim may be just a foot below the surface.

Handlers must always be aware of the potential for more avalanches. They should plan escape routes ahead of time and be prepared to respond quickly if they receive an avalanche warning.

WORKING AN AVALANCHE SCENE AT NIGHT

Night avalanche work has its own hazards. Base camp must maintain close contact with each handler. By the time the noise of an avalanche reaches the handler, it may be too late.

Use headlamps on night searches, which will leave both of your hands free. Use marker wands with reflective tape wound around them that can be easily spotted by the digging party (even a flashlight stuck in the snow will do).

> *Your attitude will be reflected in your dog's performance. If you lack confidence, your dog will know it and feel it. If you are unsteady or unnerved, your dog will be also. Your lack of confidence in yourself, your dog or the situation will result in poor performances by both of you. Go into missions well trained and with the positive attitude, "I'll find the missing person if humanly possible," and you will. Your own attitude could save a life.*

Finding deceased subjects should present no problem for the wilderness search dog. This dog indicates the remains of a pilot in a crashed aircraft. *Emil Pelcak*

14

Cadaver Training

Well-trained air-scenting dogs are highly effective in locating human remains weeks—even months—after the subject's death. All wilderness dogs should be expected to indicate both live and dead subjects. When beginning most searches, of course, dog handlers have no idea whether they are looking for a subject who is still alive or already dead. While all handlers hope to save lives, locating a deceased subject can ease a family's uncertainty and resolve an ambiguous situation for the responsible agency. To ensure continued success on future searches, your dog must be rewarded with equal play and enthusiasm whether she finds a live subject or a dead one. If your dog is sufficiently rewarded, she will be extremely reliable on both live and dead finds.

Training for Wilderness Body Searches

This section refers to missing or lost person searches conducted in remote or rural areas where the fate of the subject is unknown. ARDA has discovered one proven method for training dogs to find bodies on such searches: Train them well to find people. Although most handlers only have the opportunity to train on live subjects, their dogs respond eagerly and confidently to human scent even when a person is deceased.

While the dog's alert, initial close-in and indication should be the same as on a live subject, inexperienced dogs will sometimes exhibit caution or hesitation when they get *very close* to a decomposed body. When an inexperienced dog approaches within a foot or two of the body, she may stop and cautiously stretch her neck to sniff the body. Clearly, the dog senses that there is something different about this body. Occasionally, with an agency's permission, you may be allowed to bring nearby dogs in to acquaint them with the sight and scent of a deceased subject, particularly if there is some level of decomposition. If this can be done discreetly, your dogs first such introduction can be a positive experience if you reward her or at least praise her if a play session would be inappropriate. You may also be able to work sites where a body has just been removed since the soil may retain scent for an extended period of time.

The future success of the dog depends upon her handler's positive reinforcement. An example of the damage done if dogs aren't properly rewarded occurred on a search when one dog found a body and was immediately kenneled—without reward—because the searchers overreacted. This dog's training was set back months as it took a great deal of effort to overcome his loss of confidence and enthusiasm. If you reflect negative emotions, your dog will think she has done something wrong. If, on the other hand, your dog gets an immediate reward, she will develop a "feel-right attitude."

Training Forensic Cadaver Dogs

This section addresses training your dog to locate *forensic cadaver material*. This includes buried bodies, bone, body fluids and small pieces of tissue. This kind of training may be applied in criminal or missing-person cases where body parts are scattered over a wide area or buried, or in disaster situations where human remains may be on or under debris. Searches include those made of burned or collapsed structures.

INTRODUCING A YOUNG PUPPY TO CADAVER TRAINING

Training for this work may begin with a young puppy, but only to introduce and imprint the basics. A puppy is not going to be mentally mature enough—or experienced enough—to handle the advanced steps of cadaver training. Still, a puppy can begin to learn commands and the concept of close searching. If you are also training your dog for wilderness searches, ensure the cadaver command is distinct from the wilderness Go find. Forensic cadaver work requires a close, methodical "evidence" type of search. You should choose an appropriate command, such as Look for it, Seek, or Search.

When you teach a very young puppy the cadaver search command, you should make training into a fun game. You can train in the house during bad weather or at night. You can either hide the puppy's favorite toy or small amounts of food, such as hot dogs. Whichever reward you use, make sure it's easily accessible and placed on the floor to encourage the puppy to work with her nose down. Command her to Look for it (or whatever command you have chosen). If you use food, it will obviously be self-rewarding. If you use a toy, you can reward your puppy by playing with the toy or give her food to introduce the concept of a food reward. Regardless of the training aid you use, your puppy must be successful and have a positive experience. This training is simply imprinting the cadaver search command that tells the dog to put her nose down and work slowly. At this young age—particularly if you are also training for wilderness searches—do not overdo cadaver training. You do not want a wilderness search dog to become too ground-oriented when she works an air-scenting problem. Right now, you are simply introducing a basic concept.

Once your dog is sufficiently mature (around six months, on average), has received basic obedience training and has attained the intensity and focus required, you must decide which "find" indication will work best. Indications may be passive (lying down, sitting) or active (barking, digging or the recall/refind).

When you begin cadaver work—particularly if you have a high-drive dog—using food is both permissible and recommended for the passive alert . Using food reward helps keep the dog calm and stationary while she learns the Down or Sit indication. When she is consistently holding the Down while you approach, you can revert to the normal play reward. A food reward is *not* recommended for disaster missions, since food strewn around the site could distract the dog and enable her to reward herself, thus seriously affecting her work reliability.

If you use play instead of food in initial training, it should be more subdued than the strong play session you use for wilderness work. You want your dog to remain relatively calm. Again, in the first stages of training, you want your dog to remain beside the cadaver scent article; once you

Containers must allow scent flow, such as these knee-high hose. Note that gloves are used by the person handling the materials. *Emil Pelcak*

Human blood placed on cloth and buried for cadaver training. *Penny Sullivan*

have completed each training session, you can reward her with an animated play session.

CADAVER TRAINING AIDS

Before you begin this training, you will need cadaver material (bone, tissue, hair, teeth, body fluids) and containers.

Cadaver training aids must be handled with extreme care, both to prevent scent contamination and for the safety of the handler and assistants. People handling training aids should always wear rubber or latex gloves. Store the aids in leak-proof containers that will also protect them from cross-contamination. Some training aids—such as tissue—can be frozen to preserve longevity.

When you use the aids during training sessions, make sure they are kept in containers that will prevent the dog from destroying or ingesting them, and reduce the risk to handlers and assistants.

Commonly-used containers include PVC pipe or plastic tubes, which can also serve as the dog's retrieve toy. Other possible containers include glass jars, cinderblocks (which can be set out in a line, with one block containing cadaver scent and the other ones empty), knee-hi's or pantyhose, and rubber hoses—anything that will allow scent to flow from it. As your training progresses, it is important to "proof" the dog by varying the containers to ensure she indicates the cadaver scent rather than the scent of the container.

Training the Passive Alert

When deciding which alert indication to use—passive or active—you must decide which works best for you and your dog, as well as its impact on evidence. The passive alert will not disturb any evidence and there are some instances where law enforcement authorities do not want the dog barking and calling attention to the find. However, if you use the passive alert, you will have to keep your dog in sight at all times. On the other hand, some dogs are so eager they dig even without training and are "naturals" for the active alert. The final decision is yours, based on the situations you may face and the natural inclinations of your dog.

Before training the passive alert, your dog must already know the obedience commands Sit and Down. Teaching your dog these commands at the same time as cadaver work will only make her confused and frustrated. While either the Sit or Down will work equally well, we will use Down in this book. If you prefer Sit, simply substitute that command.

All foundation work will be done on lead to ensure you have total control over the training exercise. Training without a leash should only be done when the dog is reliable and consistent in her Down indication. Food rewards should be hot dogs or cheese, cut into tiny pieces (about the size of a nickel), since your dog will be fed often. As mentioned earlier, we recommend using food to begin training for passive alerts, because a toy may cause your dog to become so excited that she breaks the Sit or Down before you can reach the "find."

The indication will first be taught on a training aid such as a glove or a piece of leather (without cadaver scent). Your initial goal is simply to train for the proper response. Since the purpose of this exercise is to introduce your dog to the response, it will *not* involve search work, but rather a line-of-sight exercise similar to the runaway for wilderness airscenting. This exercise serves as the basis for all future training, so that you can avoid errors when the cadaver scent is introduced.

When you go to the training area, be sure you have all the required aids: the glove or piece of leather, a 15-foot leash, and, preferably, an assistant. The area should be open so that the dog can see the article when it is thrown. Again, for purposes of this book, we will assume that you have an assistant.

It is important to realize your dog will most likely need some assistance during the first couple of tosses, or until she understands what to expect. If she runs past the article or wants to play with it, have your assistant place some pieces of food next to the article after it hits the ground. This should slow your dog enough to give her the Down command. You can place food next to the article until your dog understands there is a reason to stop at the article. It may take several sessions before she understands what is expected of her.

1. While the dog is on leash, the assistant entices her with the training article, but only enough to get her excited and not overly-stimulated.

2. The assistant then tosses the article approximately 10 feet in

Begin cadaver training with a leather article.
Garrett Dyer

front of the dog. Within seconds of the article hitting the ground, send the dog with the appropriate command ("Look for it!", "Seek!", etc.).

3. As the dog goes out, allow the leash to lightly flow through your hand. The distance the article is tossed can be shortened if the dog does not go out immediately.

4. As soon as the dog reaches the article, give the Down command.

5. When your dog is down by the article, give her calm verbal praise (again, you don't want to excite her to the point where she breaks the Down) or, if your dog is clicker trained, reward her with the clicker. If the dog gets up, give the Search command again, redirect the dog to the article, and give the Down command.

6. Approach your dog calmly—but rapidly, because you want the reward to come quickly. Once you reach your dog, give her the food reward next to the article. As stated earlier, the food should be cut into small pieces that can be given quickly and often. You should stand slightly behind your dog's head, where you can drop more small pieces of food next to the scent article from over her head. Do this until your dog focuses on the article and expects the reward to "come" from the article. This requires quickness on the part of the handler—it doesn't usually take dogs long to figure out where their food is *really* coming from (you), and you want your dog to consider the article her source for the reward.

The handler stands just behind the dog's head and quickly drops bits of food next to the scent article. *Garrett Dyer*

The purpose of continuous feeding with small pieces is to encourage the dog to remain in the Down as long as possible. Once the dog is calm, your assistant can remove the training article while you give the dog several more pieces of food. This prevents the dog from trying to play with the article—which she won't be allowed to do when actual cadaver articles are introduced.

Repeat this exercise five times in succession. After the last session, you can reward your dog by playing with her favorite toy.

Once your dog goes to the tossed article, gives the indication behavior (the Down), and remains calm and

INTRODUCING CADAVER SCENTS

Our knowledge of the true components of human scent is so limited that the use of simulated or synthetic cadaver scent material is questionable. In using such substances, you may risk inadvertently training the dog to search for nonhuman chemical odors.

The cadaver scent source should be in a container that is easily tossed and will allow the scent to flow. An assistant should be used during this exercise so you will not have to handle both the cadaver container and the food reward. Obviously, if you handle the food and then touch the container, the cadaver scent will be contaminated by the food odor. Wear gloves at all times when you handle the container.

Another important point: ARDA handlers never substitute dead animal parts for human scent under any circumstances. To use animal meat is to invite serious problems on a search. This is particularly true in disaster and drowning searches, where valuable time can be lost or divers jeopardized in attempts to recover dead deer and other animals.

stationary, the goal of this exercise has been accomplished. It is now time to replace the training article with the cadaver scent source. You will follow the same progression steps as you did with training on the article. Remember to keep your dog on leash in all the foundation exercises.

The following steps transfer your dog from the training article to indicating and searching for actual cadaver material. Obviously, the amount of time it takes to complete these steps will vary, as the dog must thoroughly understand each step.

1. This exercise is conducted in the same way as the exercise with the non-cadaver training aid. The assistant entices your dog with the cadaver scent container, and then tosses it 10 feet. Release the dog immediately. At this stage, she may not give the trained indication (Down) because she is interested in this new scent. Be patient and give your dog assistance, but do not allow her to physically interact with the container before cueing her Down. The dog should understand the concept of this training exercise, based on her previous work with the training aid. The only change in the "game" is the cadaver scent. As with the training aid, give your dog a lot of low-volume praise and the chosen reward, but only after she has completed the indication behavior.

2. If your dog responds to this exercise the same way she did with the training article, and if she consistently gives the Down indication, you may

The dog is allowed to watch as the assistant tosses the scent tube. *Garrett Dyer*

This dog gives the passive Down indication beside the scent tube. *Garrett Dyer*

remove the leash for the remaining exercises. (Many trainers continue to work dogs on leash until they reach the level of working "blind" problems, as this ensures they can maintain control over the exercises). You should increase the distance you throw the cadaver container by five-yard increments until you reach a distance of about 20 yards. Once your dog runs to the container consistently and gives the desired indication, you can begin to train her to locate the container by using her nose.

3. In this step, your dog uses her nose to search for the cadaver scent. Your assistant will entice the dog with the container, tossing it about 15 yards into a grassy area. The grass should be about two feet high—tall enough to hide the container from the dog's view, but low enough for you to watch the dog work. The enticement increased your dog's play/prey drive and now the tall grass will develop her hunt drive. Send your dog on the Search command downwind of the container. She should continue searching until she finds the container and gives the proper indication. If your dog hesitates on the indication, cue her to give the proper response and then give her the food reward. Repeat this exercise three times in succession. Once your dog is successful all three times, give her a good play session with her favorite toy.

4. After your dog successfully completes the previous three Steps, extend the distance the container is tossed to 25 yards. This is also the time to turn the dog in a circle after the container lands. This will disorient your dog so that she has to hunt for the container. At this point, the container can be thrown into wooded areas and areas containing debris.

5. After throwing the container while your dog watches, take her out of the area briefly. When you bring her back, send her on the Search command. If your dog searches for the container, finds it and then gives the proper indication, she is ready for advanced work.

Advanced Cadaver Training

At this point, your dog will be required to search for the cadaver container without seeing it placed. Advanced cadaver training begins by continuing with Step 5, above. After every five to seven exercises gradually increase the time delay before you send your dog to Search. When your dog is successful after a delay of an hour or more, she is ready to work blind problems. During this entire training session, do not hesitate to give your dog assistance when she needs it. You are *training* her, not *testing* her. Also, do not get into the "let's see what my dog can do" mindset and try to move her forward too fast; a bad problem can set your training back days—even weeks. Take your time. As with wilderness searching, final success rests on having a firm foundation.

1. Have the cadaver container placed in the training area before your dog arrives there. The cadaver container should be left in place between 30 minutes and an hour before the dog begins to search. The container should be tossed into the area, so the dog has to find it by air-scenting rather than by following the assistant's track.

2. Bring your dog into the search area, take her leash off downwind of the container and give her the Search command. The dog should continue to search until she finds the container and gives the appropriate indication. If the dog has problems because of wind shift, you can assist her by directing her into the general area. However, allow your dog to make the find.

3. Extend the time the container is placed prior to bringing your dog into the area. Do this every five to seven successful sessions. Your dog should search with enthusiasm, locate the container and give the trained indication consistently with minimal assistance. Continue increasing the time until she can successfully search for the container several days after it was placed.

4. At this point, your dog has been searching for cadaver scent on the surface. Now you can train her to find buried cadaver material by going back to basic training. Your assistant places the container a few inches beneath some vegetation. Allow the dog to observe the container being hidden. Once the assistant steps back, send your dog to search for and indicate the container in her usual manner. If necessary, help your dog the first few times while she is learning that cadaver scent can be *under* things as well as on the surface. Once your dog easily locates the container when it is underneath vegetation, you can bury the container below a few inches of soil.

5. When your dog understands that scent can be both *on* and *under* surfaces, begin working blind problems on buried scent. When you set up these problems, dig several holes and make sure the empty holes don't have cadaver scent residue. The purpose of this is to ensure your dog is alerting on cadaver scent, not on disturbed soil.

6. Once your dog is working blind problems, she can learn the Show me command. Use this command when you ask your dog to pinpoint the scent source. She should touch the source with her nose. This command can be taught as a separate exercise—use the command Show me and encourage your dog to indicate with her nose—or as part of the regular cadaver training exercise if she is reliably searching for and indicating the cadadver material.

The dog watches an assistant bury the scent tube under vegetation. *Garrett Dyer*

7. Vary your training areas. Put the cadaver scent in vehicles, buildings, debris piles—even elevated off the ground. Remember that your dog may need your assistance with each new situation until she completely understands what you expect of her.

Active Indication Training

If you are also training your dog for disaster work, DO NOT USE the dig/scratch/bark alert for cadavers, since disaster teams use this to indicate live finds. For those who want a more active alert and are not training for disaster, the active indication requires a strong desire from the dog to reach the scent source.

To get the focus and intensity necessary for active indication, you must motivate your dog to want the cadaver odor. Use one or two tubes of cadaver material to motivate your dog and make her obsessed with the cadaver scent source. *It is assumed the dog already has a strongly developed play drive.* You can achieve the initial motivation by placing the cadaver scent in plastic tubes. If your dog is reluctant to carry the plastic, you can place the scent in one of her toys. If she eagerly plays with the tubes, use them for all her training.

1. Initially, you should toss the tubes into an open field. You want to build your dog's motivation through relatively easy problems. Once your dog eagerly retrieves the scent tubes, you can toss them into tall grass or wooded areas where she has to use her nose to locate them.

2. When your dog eagerly retrieves the scent tube, you can teach her the digging/scratching indication. Train this alert by using a scratch box. If you also want to train your dog to bark, you can encourage her to Speak as she digs and tries to retrieve the tube. Many vocal dogs bark out of frustration when they can't reach the tube.

   A scratch box is made of any solid material, and contains a door that slides open—enabling the dog to retrieve the tube— or slides closed to increase her intensity by temporarily frustrating her attempts to retrieve the tube. The door should be slanted so that the dog's paws slip off easily and encourage her to dig. If your dog can't dig easily, she may bite at the box or tube. Drill several holes into the bottom of the scratch box to allow for scent flow.

   Using a scratch box requires an assistant be present. Begin scratch box training with your dog on her leash about 10 feet away from the box. The assistant entices the dog with the scent tube, then raises the box door and tosses the tube inside.

   As soon as the tube is in the box, send your dog on the cadaver command. As she approaches the box, have your assistant slide the door closed. The dog should sniff the box at the holes in the bottom of the door. As soon as she gives the indication desired by scratching or digging at the door, your assistant should open the door and allow her to retrieve the tube. Immediately praise your

The dog must become obsessed with getting the tube containing cadaver material.
Doug Teeft

Use the scratch box to develop the active bark/dig indication. *Jennifer Little*

dog, repeating this exercise three to five times in a row. It is important that you don't praise your dog too much when she approaches the box. You don't want to distract her from performing the desired indication.

Your assistant plays a passive role once he places the tube in the box. If the dog seems confused, your assistant can open and close the door slightly to attract her attention, but he must not distract the dog from the box or make her lose her focus.

Once your dog understands where the scent source is located and how to gain access to it, her behavior will intensify. Continue with this exercise until your dog consistently digs and/or scratches with the intensity desired.

3. When your dog is eagerly scratching for the cadaver scent and giving a strong dig/scratch indication, you can change the environment where you hide the tube. You can place the tube under debris or anything else that makes the dog dig or scratch.

4. For now, your dog's reward has been to retrieve the tube. But once she indicates with the desired intensity, you will have to switch to a secondary reward. This switch is necessary so that your dog doesn't pick up cadaver items on actual missions. The secondary reward can be a favorite toy, a stick or a game of tug-of-war.

This dog is giving an active dig indication. Note that the handler is using a probe. *Emil Pelcak*

Dog being scented on suitcase that contained remains of homicide victim. *Penny Sullivan*

Incorporating the secondary reward requires precise timing and accuracy. The cadaver scent should be located in an area where your dog can give the trained indication, but can't gain access to the tube. The scratch box can be used for this activity, with your assistant placing the tube in the box and closing the door again. Release the dog on the Search command and follow her, being careful not to distract her. Once your dog gives the dig/scratch indication, throw the secondary reward *toward the scent source*. It is your intention to convince the dog that the reward is coming from the box. If she realizes the reward comes from you, she may break off her indication and focus on you. Practice this exercise until the reward is delivered quickly and accurately.

5. When your dog gives the desired indication and is rewarded with a toy or stick, she can begin locating the scent coming from beneath the surface. Place your dog on leash, allowing her to watch as the assistant buries the cadaver tube. As you begin this training, you want your dog to watch so she understands where the scent tube is placed. Once the tube is buried a few inches beneath the surface, send the dog on the Search command and allow her to perform the dig/scratch indication. Use the same increasing

Well-trained dogs have proven effective at finding human bones, including these of a subject deceased several years. *Penny Sullivan*

time delays that are used in training for the passive alert. Gradually extend the time before bringing in the dog to search the area.

Once your dog learns cadaver material can be located beneath the surface and shows consistent indication behavior, begin working on more challenging problems. Bury the tube deeper and leave it in place for gradually increasing time spans before bringing your dog in to search for it.

If your dog loses her focus or intensity at any time, return to simpler problems that reinforce your earlier training.

Forensic Cadaver Searching

The earlier section in this chapter on wilderness body searching refers to finding entire bodies on a standard wilderness search, often for a lost person who has died of hypothermia as opposed to a homicide victim. The forensic cadaver search refers to finding human *evidence*, which can include buried bodies, body parts or body fluids—any human remains, large or small.

The forensic cadaver search is used for such events such as homicides where the body may be buried, has totally decomposed—or major disasters where the only remains found may be tiny fragments of tissue, bone or body fluids. Because the dog is looking for small amounts of scent, she must work very slowly and methodically with her nose close to the ground.

A dog indicates the remains of a house fire victim. *Emil Pelcak*

A dog indicates the remains of a homicide victim during a landfill search. *Peggy Stanton*

In a forensic cadaver search, the search area can be broken down into small segments that are approximately 30 to 40 yards square. Remember to pay close attention to wind direction. If you are training your dog for cadaver work at large disaster sites, she will need to become accustomed to working with close focus despite the distractions of many people nearby or noisy machinery.

Many homicide victims are found in graves that are only a few feet deep. These searches haven't necessarily presented a problem for cadaver dogs. Handlers should spend some time researching the ways that earth is disturbed at typical burial sites. The ground over a deep grave frequently shows a depression resulting from ground that settles as a body decomposes. Turning the soil and uprooting the original vegetation will also often create a visible difference between the grave and the immediate vicinity. ARDA experiments have shown that soil retains the scent of body fluids for an extended period of time. Dogs have alerted on such sites months after a body was removed.

A dog team works in mud and water while they search for victims of a gas pipeline explosion.
Emil Pelcak

*Forensic cadaver dogs can be invaluable assets when you are search-
ing for human bones, body fluids, body parts and tissue fragments
during criminal, missing-person and disaster missions.*

The dog must work independently on disaster missions. Turkey eathquake, 1999. *The Fairfax County Urban Search and Rescue Team, VA-TF1* l

15

Disaster Training

The term "disaster" brings to mind many images. Disasters can be natural or man-made: earthquakes that topple entire cities; raging flood waters that break levees and swamp whole towns; a gas leak that destroys a single-family dwelling; a major train derailment; the havoc wreaked by tornadoes; the scattered remains of a broken jumbo jet; or, as we have so tragically seen, the devastation of a massive terrorist attack.

Disaster work is never a one-person show—too many resources are involved. When search dog teams deal with collapsed structures, they must work closely with structural experts and medical trauma teams, as well as heavy-rescue specialists who are experienced with trench and confined-space rescues. It is crucial that all members of the team recognize their abilities and limitations and fully understand the interdependence of everyone. Disasters truly highlight the fact that dogs are only one part of the search and rescue equation—yes, a highly efficient and valuable part, but truly only one part of the total effort.

The see-saw is ideal for teaching a dog to control his balance when rubble shifts.
James Pearson

Disaster Sites

Whatever the particulars, a disaster is usually sudden, calamitous and very often involves a number of human victims. Dog teams may be requested to search for possible survivors buried beneath tons of debris or to help recover bodies over a large expanse of ground. In addition to the myriad scents and contamination that are present in most disaster areas, many human remains may be charred or decomposing.

Hazards abound for both dog and handler at disaster sites. There may be debris hanging above and rubble shifting below; gas leaks, toxic smoke and spills; open electrical circuits; hidden fires; razor-sharp edges; suffocating dust; and deep, miring mud. Improvisation and common sense are the rule. Obviously, every site must be approached with caution. Disaster searches must be slow and deliberate, with safety uppermost in every searcher's mind.

The rescuers' safety is always paramount and dog handlers should be familiar with the dangers inherent in disaster sites. They need to receive field and class-room training in hazardous material and basic rescue procedures, as well as conduct joint training exercises with other resources. In the field, handlers must continually rely upon the knowledge of others, especially to assess building safety and to perform proper shoring procedures. If a structural safety specialist says "Stay out," he means it! Do not endanger yourself, your dog or others by taking unnecessary risks. Your job is to work as an integral part of the team—to save and *protect* lives.

ITEMS NEEDED AT A DISASTER SITE

Carry very little on your person at the site—as every bulge can be dangerous, potentially snagging on debris.

Small radios—in slings, special pockets or a fanny pack—as well as flashlights or headlamps, are essential. Also bring small canteens of water for your dog and a protective dust mask or a respirator for yourself, as well as some food, a multi-purpose tool and first-aid supplies.

Handlers must wear nonrestrictive but protective clothing that won't become easily snagged. Hardhats (with chin straps and very little brim), work gloves and steel-toed boots are also required.

Training for Disaster Work

Training dogs for work at disaster sites is very specific. While you may apply many of the exercises used to train a wilderness search dog, additional training is required. This is particularly true if you want to join a Federal Emergency Management Agency (FEMA) or state search and rescue task force.

The scope and frequency of disasters in the United States led to the establishment of the FEMA Urban Search and Rescue System, with task forces set up around the country. In addition, several states have established their own teams, which operate separately from the federal government but generally use the same training and certification guidelines. Each task force consists of collapse rescue specialists, medical personnel, hazardous materials technicians, structural engineers and search specialists—both canine and technical. Technical search specialists—who operate fiber optic cameras and listening devices—work closely with the dog handlers.

The canine teams must pass a series of certification tests for either Level II (basic) or Level I (advanced), which include obedience, agility, direction

A disaster dog must learn to look before he leaps. *James Pearson*

and control, the live victim bark indication and rubble pile search. This chapter covers much of the training required for these teams. However, if you would like more information, you can visit FEMA's website at www.fema.gov. For information on state teams, contact your state office of emergency services.

Live-Find Dogs

The chaos of a disaster scene places many demands on search dogs. Since time is critical in searching for survivors trapped in rubble, many dogs are trained to search for live humans and to ignore the deceased. The live-find dog—using air-scent training as his foundation—must also ignore people working in the area and concentrate instead on finding the scent of people trapped alive beneath buildings and debris.

Live-find dogs work off-lead, without a collar or anything that could snag on the many hazards in a debris pile. Due to safety considerations and the often elusive qualities of the victims' scent at a disaster scene, the dog is trained to give a bark alert as close as possible to a victim's scent, summoning the handler to his side. The recall/refind is not used due to the many hazards dogs face when they move through the rubble.

The Ideal Canine Candidate

As with any search work, your dog's correct mental attitude is critical. He must be comfortable on wobbly surfaces, confident around large voids, and undeterred by the confusion and noise of large groups of people and heavy equipment, as he focuses on searching for trapped victims. In addition, he must be temperamentally sound, allowing himself to be pushed, shoved, pulled or lifted from place to place. For this reason, he must be highly sociable and trustworthy around people—and he must be able to handle the stress of a disaster situation. People sometimes claim disaster dogs are "depressed" when they encounter deceased subjects. However, ARDA's experience has shown that dogs are more likely picking up on the mental attitude of their handlers or are just tired. A well-trained, well-motivated dog is more interested in getting his reward than in the condition of the strangers he finds.

Physically, disaster dogs must be able to handle the stress of working long hours (12-hour shifts are normal) under extremely difficult conditions. While injuries to search dogs can and do occur, the physical conditioning of the dog helps prevent a minor injury from becoming a serious one. Handlers should always be alert to the physical condition of their dogs. Because foot injuries are among the most common—due to working in areas littered with shattered glass and other twisted, sharp debris—disaster dogs should have well-formed paws with thick pads. Dogs rarely wear booties while they work because they can easily lose their grip on dangerous surfaces.

The ideal canine candidate for disaster work is the same as for wilderness searching. Dogs should be sociable and have strong play, prey and hunt drives. These provide all the necessary motivation for successful training. The best reward for disaster dogs is a game of tug. Tossing a ball or a stick is too dangerous in a rubble field.

Element Training For Disaster Dogs

Disaster training requires specialized skills, as indicated in the five elements set forth in this section. However, it's advantageous for disaster dogs to have previous wilderness training where the scent flow is less complicated and more direct. In wilderness training, dogs can more easily follow the scent cone to its source to receive their reward, so handlers are able to deeply ingrain the concept of search and reward. Wilderness training also extends the dog's endurance and his willingness to work for extended periods of time.

Although you can introduce a very young puppy to disaster training with simple runaways to the edge of a small debris pile, serious training should not be undertaken until the dog is physically and mentally mature enough to successfully learn the five elements listed below. Needless to say, very young puppies should not be worked on difficult agility or search problems. You *can* introduce them to the basics as long as it is done in a fun and safe manner. It's best to spend your time with a puppy by following the wilderness training steps, described in previous chapters, that will build his play drive and teach him to air scent.

The five required elements in this section are: obedience and control, agility, the directed send, the bark/live-find indication, and rubble search. Each of these elements has a *specific objective* that contributes to the development of a dog who can search disaster areas in a safe, effective, independent and confident manner. These elements are also used for FEMA disaster dog certification.

OBEDIENCE AND CONTROL

Control is essential in disaster work, and from a safety standpoint, it is critical. Control can and should be taught in several exercises prior to—and in conjunction with—search training.

All control is based on general obedience training. This control is particularly important in agility training, where an instant response to obedience commands may be required to prevent injury. The dog should be obedient to the commands Heel on and off-leash, Sit, Down, Stay and Come, as well as an emergency stop

Dogs must not show aggression toward other people or dogs during the Figure 8 exercise. *Penny Sullivan*

Dogs must learn to go through tunnels and voids. *James Pearson*

command such as Wait. Obedience can be taught using play or food rewards, but it must always be done with positive reinforcement. A dog with a particularly high play drive may respond better to a food reward so that he doesn't become so excited with play that he loses focus on obedience training.

Control commands practiced during agility should include Wait, Easy, Turn Around, Stop and Stay. The dog should respond immediately, without hesitation. In addition, introduce hand signals since, in many disaster situations, handlers cannot be heard over the noise at the site and dogs must be controlled without verbal commands. (See "Using Both Verbal and Hand Signals" in the Directed Send section).

Above all, exercises must be *fun* for your dog so he is ready to search with great eagerness yet remain under control. During obedience and control training, your dog will learn he should look to you for direction and physical assistance. If you frighten him in this early stage of training, you will find it difficult—if not impossible—to develop a truly reliable disaster search dog.

Once your dog is reliable on basic commands, he must learn to obey them and disregard other dogs, people, loud noise or heavy machinery. FEMA certification requires dogs to heel through, as well as perform a Figure 8 around, other people and dogs. It is critical your dog be under complete control both on and off-leash He must not show any aggression toward other people or dogs.

The time you spend now on obedience training will pay dividends on actual missions. During briefings or while you wait to board an airplane you will routinely use the Long down. You will constantly have your dog Heel in airports and hotels, as well as when you are going to and from the disaster site. An immediate response to the Stop, Down or Wait commands is critical, since disaster sites are extremely dangerous. Shifting rubble, sudden fires and high ledges are common—you must be able to stop your dog instantly.

Aggression toward people and dogs cannot be tolerated. FEMA and state teams specifically test for this trait because their dogs are expected to travel in close quarters, work near other teams and represent the task force at ceremonies and other special occasions. The dogs are frequently the center of attention and need to be able to handle stress without showing any aggression.

AGILITY

As with obedience training, all agility training will be tested on an actual mission. Ladder training is critical because transport may be by airplane with steep, grated steel ladders providing the only access available to the plane. Ladders may also provide the only access to some parts of a debris pile. See-saw training is invaluable when rubble shifts, as the dog has learned how to ride out the shift and then continue to search. Your dog must learn to handle heights through training exercises such as crossing an elevated plank. His ability to crawl through narrow spaces and tunnels will be tested, since these abound at disaster sites—and dogs are often the only ones able to enter and search these voids. A disaster mission is not the appropriate time to realize your dog needs more training.

The basics of agility training described in Chapter 4 must be mastered before your dog can safely perform advanced disaster work. Even after agility training, however, your dog must learn to improve control over his body in order to be safe in the disaster environment. To counter the normal response of jumping off moving or

A swinging bridge helps teach the dog how to handle shifting surfaces. *Tony Campion*

Dogs must become accustomed to heights during agility training. *Jane Adair*

Dogs must be confident on unstable surfaces. *James Pearson*

shifting debris, he must learn to use his body weight to keep his balance. As stated above, the see-saw obstacle is one of the best for teaching this kind of control as it requires your dog to stop on the see-saw and move slowly even when the see-saw tips.

In addition, your dog must be confident on elevated objects (both wide and narrow platforms), unpleasant surfaces (rough or slick), and when entering or exiting dark tunnels and low crawl spaces. It is very important your dog learns how to negotiate ladders. While the normal agility ladder is relatively easy to climb, disaster dogs may have to climb up or down a very steep ladder set at a 45° angle or more, with flat or round rungs. To climb this kind of ladder your dog must learn exactly where to place his hind feet. He can't rely on the natural impulse to pull and direct his body using his front legs. Be sure your dog is adept and confident on easy ladders before starting him on more difficult ones.

While play reward is appropriate on some individual obstacles and after completing the entire course, food reward may be more useful on obstacles where you want to reward your dog immediately without getting him so excited he loses his footing or falls.

THE DIRECTED SEND

Although your dog is expected to work independently and range freely over rubble, there are times—due to weather conditions or safety factors—when you must be able to direct him to search a specific area from a distance. The dog needs to be able to follow directions to go left, right, back and forward. The directions do not need to be precise, because he must pick his own way safely across the rubble, but they must be followed immediately. Not only is this necessary when searching a particular area, but you may see a safety hazard your dog does not recognize. You must be prepared to direct your dog away from such hazards. The basic control command for directed search is Wait. Once your dog stops and is watching you, he can be directed with additional signals.

While there are many ways to train a dog to obey direction commands for disaster work, tapping into his play drive creates the necessary motivation for this work. It can also make the commands more solid under the stressful conditions of an actual mission. As with any training, timing is very important. Initially, it is critical to reward your dog when he moves in the requested direction. You can add the Wait command later, which should be trained separately. (There are many opportunities for this training, including during agility work, while climbing up or down stairs, going through doors or getting in and out of cars and crates.)

Using Both Verbal *and* Hand Commands

Both verbal and hand commands must be learned. There will be instances in a disaster when your dog must be directed by verbal commands. These include a forward command (usually Go or Go out), an up command (usually Hup), a back command, and commands to move left or right. Select words you will remember in an emergency situation. In other cases, the noise at a disaster site will be so loud that you can only use hand signals. Teach all of these commands during agility training, wilderness work and even when you are throwing a toy.

How you train your dog for hand signals depends upon what works best for you and your dog. Some trainers begin with verbal commands and add hand signals only when the dog is solid on the verbal commands, but most introduce both simultaneously, giving the verbal command and hand signal from the very beginning. If you choose the latter, you must give the hand signal at precisely the same moment as the verbal command.

The most commonly used hand signals are:

- Holding your arm and hand extended straight out in front of you for Forward (Go or Go out)

- The arm extended forward with the hand raised, palm toward the dog, for Wait

- Raising one or both arms straight up over your head for Back

- Extending your arm and hand straight out to the side for Left or Right

Vary the commands when you are training for the directed send. Use only the verbal commands on some occasions. On others use only hand signals, and on yet others, combine the two. Your dog must be reliable with both.

A disaster task force tests a dog's directed send skill through what is commonly referred to as "canine baseball," where the dog is directed to objects (often raised pallets) set out in the shape of a baseball diamond. This diamond includes the pitcher's mound, first, second and third bases, and home plate (where the handler stands during the test). The test requires the handler send his dog to the various bases—such as from home plate to third base, then to the pitcher's mound, then to second base, back to the pitcher's mound, and back to third base—then be recalled to home plate. The handler must not move beyond the eight-foot board or line that represents home plate, and he must not step over it. Obviously, this requires your dog to respond reliably to hand and verbal signals from a distance. He must also understand the Hup or On it command so that he will climb on the pallet. Once your dog is on the pallet, he must remain there for five seconds until you direct him to another base.

Sending the dog forward to the first pallet.
Garrett Dyer

To train for the Directed send, you will need four stable wooden spools (like ones used to store cables) or pallets, approximately 24 × 36 inches, and 10 to 20 inches high. For purposes of simplicity, we will use the term "pallets" to refer to both. As you begin training, place two pallets close together. As your dog learns what you expect of him, move the pallets farther apart as you also move farther from your dog, so that he learns to obey commands from a distance. Eventually,

Giving the dog the Wait command. *Garrett Dyer*

you should be able to direct your dog with the pallets placed 25 yards or more apart, and with the pitcher's mound 25 yards from where you stand at home plate.

Directed-Send Exercise A: Learning the Hup, On it, Forward, and Wait Commands:

Before you begin directed-send training, make sure your dog has a solid understanding of the Hup or On it command.

1. Use a leash to ensure control. You may lightly tap the pallet to encourage your dog to jump up on it, but you should dispense with the visual cue as soon as the dog responds reliably to the verbal command. As soon as your dog jumps on the pallet, reward him with his favorite toy.

2. Once your dog learns that jumping up on the pallet earns him his toy, you can move back a couple of yards, give the Forward and Hup commands, and immediately reward him when he jumps up on the pallet. Since you are some distance from the pallet, you must be sure the toy is thrown so it lands near your dog's head. If you throw the toy over your dog, or if he does not see it, he will not get the instant reward that is critical to his associating jumping up on the pallet with earning his toy.

3. As your dog learns the Forward command, increase the distance between you and the pallet, saying Hup as he nears the pallet to reinforce that command. Move around the pallet and send your dog from different

directions to make sure he understands that he must move to the pallet from any location on the Forward command, and to jump up on it with the Hup command.

If at any time he turns back toward you and looks for his toy before he reaches the pallet, move closer and practice making the Hup command more solid by teaching him that only jumping up on the pallet will produce his toy. If necessary, have someone hold your dog while you go up to the pallet, tap it, return to the dog, and then send him again. He needs to learn that he will only get his reward if he climbs up on the pallet. Be patient and do not rush this work.

4. Vary your commands, giving verbal commands one time, hand signals the next, and then combining the two another time.

5. Once your dog is solid on his Forward and Hup commands, you can introduce him to the Wait command. But only do this when he is on the pallet—and only do it intermittently. If your dog leaps up on the first pallet, give him the Wait command, then send him to the second pallet and reward him immediately. If his response to the Hup command slows at any point, discontinue the Wait for a few sessions. Your main goal right now is to keep this exercise fast and fun for your dog. When your dog is completely solid on the Forward and Hup commands, you can begin training the Back command.

Directed-Send Exercise B: Teaching the Back Command

The most difficult thing for a dog to master may be going away from his handler on the Back command. It is very important to take the time needed to make this direction solid through many repetitions. Dogs easily learn the Left and Right commands, so these can be taught later. The Back command needs to be isolated in training and should not be combined with the Forward, Left or Right commands until your dog fully understands the "Back" command.

1. To begin training the Back command, place your dog on the first pallet, with a second pallet a couple of yards behind it. Stand in front of the dog, give the Wait command, then walk around and tap the second pallet. Return to the front of the first pallet, ensuring the dog is facing you, and give the Back command. It is important for the dog to make an actual 180° turn to reach the second pallet. During an actual disaster, he may encounter hazards and voids by moving too much to the left or right if he has not learned to move straight back during training.

2. Once your dog is on the second pallet, reward him *immediately*. Do *not* wait for him to turn toward you.

If your dog fails to move toward the second pallet, repeat the tapping sequence until he understands what you want.

3. After your dog responds reliably by turning around and moving to the second pallet, increase the distance between the two pallets until, eventually, they are about 25 yards apart. As with the Forward command, take your time. Make sure the dog fully understands what is expected of him before you move to the next step.

Directing the dog to go Back to the second pallet. *Garrett Dyer*

4. Work your dog with both hand and verbal signals, varying their use.

5. When you are certain the dog understands the Back command and will move to the second pallet with little or no hesitation, begin sending him to the first pallet on the Forward command. At other times, work the dog solely on going back. He must be reliable with both commands.

Directed-Send Exercise C: Teaching the Left and Right Commands

Once your dog is solid on the Forward and Back commands, begin introducing both the Left and Right commands. The training steps are the same as for the Back command.

1. Start with the dog on one pallet, with another placed a few yards to the side. Move to the second pallet, tap it, return to stand in front of the dog, then send him to it (use any verbal command that works, including the words Left and Right). If the dog's work on the Hup command and previous pallet work is reliable, he should have no trouble understanding what is expected of him. Again, reward him immediately with his toy once he is on the second pallet.

2. As your dog progresses with the Left and Right commands, gradually move farther from the pallets and move the pallets farther apart. At this point, your dog should understand the exercise and you should not have to move the pallets in the small increments that were used in the previous steps.

3. As with the other exercises, introduce hand signals and vary their usage.

Directed send to the right. *Garrett Dyer*

4. When your dog clearly understands the commands and reliably responds
   to each, you can place all four pallets on the field at the 25-yard distance
   and begin practicing sending him Left, Right, Back and Forward.

Vary where you stand and the starting point for the dog. For example, you can
stand in front of first base with the dog on the Wait command at the pitcher's
mound, and then send the dog to second base. The next time, you can stand in
front of third base with the dog on the Wait command at second base, and then
send him to the pitcher's mound. If you fail to vary both your location and the dog's
starting point, you will invite pattern training where the dog is actually just following a particular routine. You want a dog who responds in any direction—from
any place—when you actually work a rubble site.

Advanced Directed-Send Exercises

When your dog is reliable in his direction work, replace the pallets with a less
obvious target, or hide the pallets in tall grass so the dog can't see the pallet unless
he follows your direction. The dog must understand that only by going in the direction you send him—even if he can't see the target—will he receive his reward.

Eventually, a person hidden in the rubble pile will provide the dog's reward.
Once he is working the pile, set up problems so that the dog picks up the victim's
scent and earns his reward by following your directions. As in all search work, disaster training instills teamwork between the dog and handler. This way, the dog
knows good things happen when he follows the commands of his handler.

Also, as with all other search work, keep direction training upbeat for the dog.
It is advisable to occasionally surprise the dog with a reward after you ask him to

move in one direction. At other times, reward him only after he moves in three or four directions. Vary the problems for the dog by standing at home plate and sending him to the pitcher's mound, then to first base, back to the pitcher's mound, then call him back to you at home plate. Occasionally, give him his reward when he jumps up on the pallet instead of giving him the Wait command. If he performs an exercise with great speed and accuracy, end the training session at that point, even if you had planned on a more extended session.

THE BARK/LIVE FIND INDICATION

The bark alert is the most effective indication of a live find. Because a handler should avoid crossing hazardous rubble unless it's absolutely necessary, the bark alert enables the handler to wait until her dog has indicated a find. If the dog is working out of the handler's sight, the bark alert will give the handler an indication of the dog's location so she can find him more quickly. This behavior can be channeled into search work once the dog knows that barking will lead to his toy reward.

Training the Bark Alert

Training the focused bark to indicate live human scent should be undertaken with great care. This indication is the critical dog behavior that determines successful disaster search dog work. Don't rush any of the steps—it is very important to build a strong foundation before you move to rubble work. Your dog should be both intensely focused and joyous in his bark indication.

Initially, the dog must learn that barking earns him his toy. You can hold the toy behind your back, under your arm or in plain sight; the one constant is that repetitive barking brings the toy to the dog. If the dog is not a natural barker, you can frustrate him by keeping the toy just out of reach until he gives the beginning sound of a bark. Immediately reward this attempt by the dog and then shape his behavior by gradually asking for stronger and more frequent barks before he gets his toy.

The dog can be held by another person or he can be tied to a fence. We recommend that the dog wear a harness or a padded agitation collar for this procedure, since you do *not* want to choke him by using a chain training collar—nothing should interfere with the dog's ability to bark.

Timing is critical throughout the development of the bark alert. The dog must be allowed to get his toy almost simultaneously with his bark so that he understands that the barking brings him his toy. Once the bark is offered reliably, you should let him have his reward on a variable reinforcement schedule (sometimes one bark earns his toy, sometimes it takes 20 barks). Variable rewards also help maintain the dog's intensity and focus—he never knows whether the next bark is the one that will earn him his toy.

Teaching a puppy to bark using a toy.
Jane Adair

The "victim" rewards the dog as soon as the dog gives the bark alert. *James Pearson*

Once your dog barks reliably for you, transfer this response to another person. Follow the same procedure, but with you holding the dog. This time, the other person has the toy and rewards the dog on the variable reinforcement schedule.

When the dog barks intensely for his reward as it is held by another person, the assistant can run a short distance away, then stop and wait for you to send the dog. The dog should run to the assistant and begin barking for his toy. The assistant should stop in various positions, such as standing, kneeling and lying down. If the dog circles the assistant and tries to grab the toy, set up the next problem so the assistant stands against a wall or a fence. The dog should only get his toy by barking at the assistant.

The Bark Barrel

The next step is to transfer the dog's bark indication to an inaccessible assistant. A bark barrel or box is used to teach the dog he is searching for inaccessible, live human scent which he must indicate by barking in order to get his reward. A person hides inside the bark barrel and the dog is trained to stay and bark at the source of human scent. Energy and enthusiasm are essential. The dog learns that his bark makes the barrel open so he can get his toy and earn a fun game of tug. Tugs or balls on string are preferred, since this skill will be transferred to the rubble, where—for obvious safety reasons—the play reward must be limited to the hidden person's location.

Construct a bark barrel by tightly joining two 55-gallon drums—fitted with a plywood door that has a handle on the *inside*, where it can be controlled by the assistant. You may also have a view window on the door so the assistant can see the dog and determine the best moment for a reward. It is important that the assistant's scent escapes only through the door, which will have small holes drilled in it to allow scent flow.

Use the bark barrel to train the bark alert by following these steps:

1. Introduce the dog to the bark barrel by throwing his toy in the opening and allowing him to retrieve it.

2. The assistant then does a runaway to the barrel and climbs inside, with the door off and to one side. He should cover the toy so the dog has to bark in order to receive it.

3. Once the assistant is in position, the dog should be sent to earn his reward by barking. Be sure to reward on only one or two barks, until the dog is sure of the behavior asked of him in this new setting.

4. Once the dog runs happily and quickly to the assistant in the barrel, use the cover to slowly close the opening. At first, the cover should conceal approximately one-quarter of the opening, then one-half, then seven-eighths. Before you cover the entire opening, the dog should be sent with the door open—then close it just before he reaches the barrel.

Each of these steps will require many repetitions. You should vary the required number of barks before you move on to the next step. Once the dog barks repetitively for the door to open with his toy, the assistant can get in the barrel before the dog is brought to the area. At this point, the dog is working blind, but this should pose no problem if the dog is well-grounded in air scenting. Once the dog is in the area, release him about 25 yards from the barrel. He should then run to the barrel, sniff for human scent and begin to bark for his toy. Again, vary the number of barks required before you give the dog his toy reward.

Some dogs are natural diggers and try to penetrate the barrel. It is very important these dogs only be rewarded on the bark and never on penetration, until their

A dog gives the bark/scratch indication at the bark barrel. *Garrett Dyer*

bark foundation is very solid. Otherwise, under stress, their natural tendency will be to dig more and bark less. For dogs who only bark, add penetration later by rewarding your dog when he additionally scratches at the barrel.

To encourage your dog to be discriminating—and not just bark at the sight of the barrel—set up three bark barrels in a row, with the assistant in only one barrel. This challenge will encourage the dog to focus on his scenting ability and not on the visual cue of the bark barrel itself.

When the dog is ready for search work, be sure to use the wind to his advantage. Take a lot of time before you increase the complexity of the scent problem. It is important to remember training should be constantly varied—some days consisting of motivational runaways, pop-ups from the rubble (where the assistant opens the lid, waves the toy, then closes the lid), or call-outs by the assistant. The dog should never think that disaster work just gets harder and harder. Remember to keep it fun for both you and the dog.

Rubble Search

Except for assessing the dog's comfort on large rubble piles, rubble search work is not started until the dog is solid on the previous skills. His confidence on obstacles and his love of the "bark and get my toy" game should now be so strong that he takes it in stride when you ask him to search across difficult voids and unpleasant footing surfaces for his reward.

When beginning a rubble search, the reward from the hidden person should come quickly. As the dog's confidence in searching increases, the reward can be given after a longer bark alert. It is important to vary the length of time before rewarding the dog, so he never knows when his toy will appear.

The bark barrel is a good tool for transferring the bark indication to the rubble pile. The dog knows he is looking for inaccessible, live human scent. Put the bark barrel on the rubble and then *go back to the beginning steps*. Since you are now asking for the bark indication in a more difficult environment, it is important to help the dog and make his task easier. As the assistant gets in the barrel, put the dog on the pile where he can watch. When the dog is sent to the barrel, the assistant should not close the lid until the dog is almost at the barrel. Ask for only one or two barks at first. The dog still needs to think that working to earn his toy is easy. Continue to use variable reinforcement regarding the number of barks you require before you give the dog his toy. When the dog is comfortable barking for his toy on the pile, increase distances, generally reduce visual cues, and use concrete culverts with lids instead of the barrel.

Victims should be hidden in holes of various lengths and depths, with multiple areas for the scent to escape. This teaches the dog to commit to different scent intensities. As the dog gains experience, he should be taught to get as close to the scent source as possible before beginning his bark indication. He must also learn to commit to a single spot once he begins his bark indication. The dog should continue barking regardless of any distractions—including the approach of his handler. His entire focus and intensity must be on the victim.

As the dog's rubble skills develop, add distractions to the environment. The dog must be able to work in the midst of people and loud noises such as generators and jackhammers.

> *These training techniques have produced highly-skilled disaster search dogs. You can never duplicate the challenges and stresses of a real disaster in training situations. However, the combination of a sound temperament, strong play and hunt drives—and well-developed training—enables a disaster search dog to transfer his skills to real-life scenarios.*

A dog searches the tangled remains of the United States Embassy in Nairobi, Kenya, after a terrorist bombing in 1998. *Garrett Dyer*

An ARDA team searches for victims of the 1985 Puerto Rican mudslides. *Bob Langendoen*

16

Disaster
Missions

Over the past thirty years, ARDA handlers have responded on numerous disaster missions, including the Johnstown, Pennsylvania floods in 1977, the Mt. St. Helens eruption in 1980, the Puerto Rican mudslides in 1985, the Soviet Armenia earthquake in 1988, and the terrorist attacks in New York and Washington. It is important to note that ARDA handlers responding on missions, including the Nairobi Embassy bombing and the September 11th attacks, did so as members of either FEMA or state urban search-and-rescue task forces, and had undergone the additional training and certification required of task force members.

Attack on the World Trade Center, September 11, 2001

It was a day most people will never forget. At 8:46 A.M. on a perfect September morning, an airliner flew into the North Tower of New York City's World Trade Center. At 9:05 A.M., as America watched in horror, a second airliner struck the South Tower.

ARDA handlers were soon activated with both the Pennsylvania and New Jersey Task Forces responding to the worst terrorist attack in American history.

The remnants of the upper part of the South Tower, now embedded in the pavement, were known to rescue workers as "the flower." *Penny Sullivan*

The twisted wreckage of the World Trade Center. *Penny Sullivan*

New York City's Office of Emergency Management reacted immediately and requested assistance for what they knew would be a disaster of unimaginable proportions. At 9:15 A.M. they contacted New Jersey Task Force 1, based in Lakehurst, New Jersey. Because of their proximity to the disaster, the New Jersey Task Force was able to respond with more equipment and manpower than usual for an Urban Task Force—including more dogs than the standard four teams.

The Task Force was bused into New York City, with an escort from the New Jersey State Police. Two tractor-trailers and an array of trucks carrying the team's equipment followed the buses. The dogs were transported on the buses, either sitting on seats next to their handlers or lying in the aisle.

The trip into the city was understandably somber. As the Team traveled up the New Jersey Turnpike and neared lower Manhattan, they could see dark smoke billowing up from the distant skyline. The attack had been so sudden and the threat so real, that many people wondered about the safety of the bridges and tunnels leading into New York City. Security was tight and the convoy was stopped at the entrance to the Lincoln Tunnel for security clearance. Handlers took advantage of this break to exercise their dogs in the few available patches of grass.

Once in midtown Manhattan, the Task Force set up operations at the Jacob Javits Convention Center. They set up tents and established separate areas for planning, operations, logistics, decontamination, dining and communications. The Task Force designated sleeping areas, giving special consideration to their dogs. Using tarpaulins as dividers, most of the handlers sectioned off their sleeping quarters so that dogs and handlers had their own separate "rooms." When the dog

A dog and handler team await their assignment at the World Trade Center. *Penny Sullivan*

A dog and handler team searching the rubble of the World Trade Center. *Andrea Booher, FEMA*

crates were set up, just enough space remained within the compartments for the handlers to sleep alongside their dogs. This was a great advantage during the course of the deployment, as the dogs had a secure, private place where they could get truly rested between assignments.

By mid-afternoon, the teams were transported to lower Manhattan, to what quickly became known as Ground Zero. The buses had to be cleared through a number of security checkpoints and could only get to within a few blocks of the site. From that point, the dog teams and other Task Force members had to make their way on foot, carrying all their necessary equipment.

The streets were littered with debris and a thick, gray ash covered everything in sight. Some vehicles were crushed while others still smoldered. Ash and smoke choked the air, making breathing difficult. Even through their masks and respirators, the handlers could smell the acrid scent. As the teams approached the site, Building 7 came crashing down not far from them in a mountain of dust and debris. The Task Force was told to stand by until the scene was safe enough to work the dogs.

Later that night, teams were finally given clearance and the dogs began searching for survivors in the massive ruins covering West Street. This was the area where many of the initial responders were caught when the towers collapsed.

At first sight, no one could comprehend the scene before them. It was utterly surreal. A mass of fallen steel columns and enormous piles of twisted metal stretched toward the skeletal remains of the twin towers and other heavily damaged buildings. The area was huge—much larger than anyone thought possible.

Giant floodlights illuminated the scene from above as hundreds of rescue workers combed through the piles. The noise from countless generators and heavy equipment was deafening. Flames from numerous fires flared up in the distance, and thick smoke and ash swirled everywhere.

The search managers were able to roughly divide the area into four quadrants, using some debris as landmarks. One of the most noticeable markers was a trio of steel beam sections standing upright and close together, off to one side. The team learned later these sections were part of the upper reaches of the South Tower, and had embedded themselves in the concrete pavement when they fell. Searchers referred to this landmark as "the flower."

Two dog teams and one safety person were assigned to each quadrant. The area was so large that teams could easily work far enough away from one another without interference. However, if one of the dogs showed some interest, the second dog could be brought over to double-check the scent. As the dogs started working, handlers removed their dogs' collars and leashes so they wouldn't get caught on the jagged steel that was everywhere.

In spite of the horrendous conditions, the dogs performed exceptionally well. When given the command to Go find, they eagerly ranged out ahead of their handlers, seeking human scent. It was quickly apparent that all their agility and directional training had paid off. The dogs climbed slick steel without hesitation. They worked their way along beams that stretched out over pits of burning debris, and made their way through jumbles of twisted metal. They worked within inches of open fires and only ignored their handlers' commands to Go back, Right or Left

Agility training pays off as this dog maneuvers among the wreckage of the World Trade Center. *Michael Rieger, FEMA*

Searching the World Trade Center site required an intense, methodical and focused effort. *Lt. Daniel Donadio, NYPD K-9*

when they encountered extreme temperatures from an intense inferno burning far beneath them.

Firefighters working the scene asked many handlers to search specific areas. In one situation, a handler sent her dog into a void, as requested. She watched her dog make his way through the debris and then disappear from sight. In instances such as this one, a handler has no idea what her dog might encounter. If the dog were to find a survivor, he would bark to alert his handler. Silence—on the other hand—could mean many things. It might mean the dog was still searching, but it also might mean that he fell into a pit, or had been trapped or injured. As time passed, the handler's concern grew. Even when she called her dog, she got no response. Finally, a firefighter crouching near the entrance to the void reported that he could see the dog making his way back toward them over the debris. Somehow, the dog had found his way out of the wreckage through a distant opening and was returning unhurt.

In another instance, one of the dogs stepped too close to a hot spot and the hair on the side of his foot caught on fire. Fortunately, his handler smothered the flames immediately. Although the dog's hair was singed, he was able to continue working.

Both of these examples provide important lessons about disaster work: While it may look glamorous from the outside, there are always heart-stopping moments for both the dog and handler. Training and physical conditioning can mean the difference between a safe search and injury—even death.

The search itself was intense, demanding and continuous. Teams hoped to rescue at least one survivor, but the dogs found only human remains. Time and again, teams were asked to check a particular location, but no one was found alive. On one occasion, a team was asked to look beneath a crushed fire truck; a dog eased his way under the mangled wreckage and began digging. With his front teeth, the dog carefully extracted what was left of a firefighter's harness—but he gave no bark alert for a live find.

Finally, the search was called off for the night and, as the teams worked their way back toward their bus, they stopped at a Humane Society trailer set up to give each dog a quick physical examination. Veterinarians and technicians flushed the dogs' eyes, washed off their paws and checked their ears. All the dogs were tired, but they were generally in good shape. Once back at the Javits Center, both dogs and handlers were able to get a well-deserved rest.

The first FEMA task forces arrived the next day. In all, FEMA rotated 21 task forces of 62 people each (including four dog/handler teams per task force) to the World Trade Center site. Considering the initial chaos that followed the attack, the overall immensity of the situation and the number of rescue personnel arriving, New York City Command did an unbelievable job. It is an especially amazing tribute to those left in charge, considering the number of key emergency administrators killed in the buildings' collapse.

Once the FEMA task forces began arriving, search personnel were divided into two 12-hour shifts. Additionally, the various urban search and rescue teams—both FEMA and state—were assigned to specific areas within the overall site. Some teams searched what remained of the twin towers themselves, while others searched surrounding areas. This included the subterranean mall beneath the towers and all the heavily damaged buildings nearby. Collateral damage was enormous—some structures, including Building 7 and the Marriott Vista Hotel— were completely destroyed.

Early on, there were fears that some of the buildings surrounding the twin towers were so badly damaged that they would collapse. Several times during the first few days—when it seemed those structures were about to come down—the call went out for everyone to flee. Handlers, dogs and everyone else were pushed into the throngs of people running to get away. Fortunately, these calls proved groundless.

In the days immediately following September 11th, the estimated number of people missing continued to climb. One of the hardest experiences for the rescue workers was telling the relatives of missing individuals that they had not seen their family members. Wives, husbands, mothers, fathers, sons and daughters all came to the site with photographs of their loved ones. They hung these photos on windows, doors, trees and lamp posts —anywhere a passerby might see a face.

Throughout its 10-day deployment, the New Jersey Task Force searched for survivors around the clock, dogs had been trained to indicate inaccessible survivors with a bark alert, but to everyone's sorrow they did not find anyone alive.

The dogs were, however, very successful at indicating human remains. During each work shift, teams were called time and again to search numerous locations throughout the pile. Firefighters and police officers—hoping to find their buried brothers—would simply ask the teams, "Please, check this out." When the dogs found remains, their body language was unmistakable. Although the majority of dogs had no previous exposure to cadaver searching, they had no trouble recognizing areas that contained buried bodies or fragments of human tissue. The dogs' entire demeanor changed as they intensely focused on one particular area. Most dogs pawed or dug gently at the spot, nosing it repeatedly with marked interest as they took in the scent. Some urinated nearby to mark a spot.

Although they weren't able to perform any rescues, the dogs were invaluable in locating the dead. It is hoped that once identified, those remains helped bring a sense of closure to grieving families.

Search dogs must maintain their focus despite distractions and bystanders. Dogs at the World Trade Center stayed on the job through the roar of heavy machinery and the heat and smoke of smoldering fires. *Lt. Daniel Donadio, NYPD K-9*

After each 12-hour shift, the handlers and dogs were bused back to the Javits Center for down time. Before changing their clothes, handlers checked their dogs for signs of injury, shampooed them thoroughly and toweled them off. They fed the dogs and walked them one more time before they put them in their crates for a much-deserved rest. Only after the dogs were taken care of would the handlers clean themselves up and get something to eat.

The outpouring of support at Ground Zero was amazing. Search teams were flooded with donated food, clothing and equipment from all over the country. Americans from every walk of life volunteered to help in any way possible. Numerous field kitchens were set up around the Javits Center and in the vicinity of Ground Zero—all the provisions and labor were completely donated. In the New Jersey Task Force Base of Operations, the Salvation Army set up an entire kitchen and food bar to feed each shift as it arrived from or departed for Ground Zero.

Supplies poured in for the dogs, as well. Dog food came by the pallet, along with everything from collars and leashes to water bowls. And booties! Somehow, word had gotten out that the search dogs needed booties, and they arrived by the hundreds. Although some dogs did in fact use booties, most handlers preferred to let their dogs work without them. Booties easily interfere with a dog's ability to "feel" and, in most instances, dogs get better traction without them.

Each day, as the Task Force made its way to the site, crowds of bystanders lined the route, waving American flags, cheering wildly and holding up hand-printed signs that said "Thank you!" Emotions ran high and, in the course of their stay, Task Force members experienced a wide range of intense feelings. These feelings were shared by all the rescue workers.

One of the most important roles the dogs performed was as therapists for the many firefighters, police officers and rescue workers. There were countless times when workers stopped to pat the dogs. Oftentimes, these workers would say how much they missed their own dogs. Or they would talk softly, holding private conversations that only they and the dog could hear. Then the worker would get down to nuzzle the dog one last time and receive a wet kiss in return. At these times, handlers realized that they weren't there only as search dog handlers, but as part of the whole human disaster experience.

The dogs handled the entire situation magnificently. Even the most experienced handlers were in awe. Most felt the training they and their dogs had received prior to September 11th was invaluable. Although nothing could prepare anyone for the conditions at the World Trade Center, going through the training steps necessary to reach the FEMA standard had prepared the teams well. In particular, the handlers agreed that time spent ensuring their dog's agility, directability and overall control was extremely useful. Dogs who are confident and sure of their footing will work safely. They can focus on their handlers' commands to Wait or Turn around when necessary to avoid injury. No matter how good their noses, if dogs are uncomfortable or worried about their own safety, they won't be able to work.

Following the deployment, handlers were asked to list some lessons learned, along with their thoughts for future improvement. They responded with the following:

- Practice giving commands while wearing a dust mask or respirator. Your dog should become familiar with the difference in your voice.

- Train with more distractions and contaminants. Especially practice working the dogs through and around large groups of people.

- Work the dogs for longer periods of time, increasing their endurance so they don't automatically expect their reward in a short time.

- Train on as many different surfaces in as many different settings as possible.

- Train with various fire departments and emergency service workers. They need to understand the dogs' capabilities and how best to use them.

- Work with various dog harnesses—practice lowering and lifting the dogs.

■ Consider Therapy Dog training for both dogs and handlers. Many of the search dogs at Ground Zero found themselves playing that role.

■ Emphasize control with agility and directional training. It is one of the most important elements of the working disaster dog.

■ Make sure you or your team carries enough of your dog's regular food. You don't want to change food in the middle of a deployment.

■ Provide crates for the dogs at the forward command post. When the dogs are not being used, they will be better able to rest.

■ While working your dog, be sure to carry ample water and a small treat for your dog *on your person*. You never know when you may not get back to your forward base for an extended period of time.

■ Do not forget to take your dog aside occasionally for a play session. It is one of the best ways to relieve stress for both you and your dog.

■ Be certain to give your dog adequate breaks at various times during each 12-hour shift. The search team might establish a schedule for the dogs, such as one hour on and 20 minutes off.

■ Keep track of the dogs' comfort while searching. Flush their eyes as necessary and keep them hydrated.

■ Arrange for alternate areas near the base of operations in which to relieve the dogs. The areas around the Javits Center were much too crowded.

■ The hazardous materials (hazmat) component of each task force should specifically take the dogs' needs into account. Dogs are close to the ground and have unique susceptibilities. The hazmat team should be prepared to set up a "doggie decon" station, as was done at one of the forward operations centers. Each task force should have a veterinarian on the roster as an integral part of the team.

■ Task forces should consider deploying more dogs per task force in the future. No leeway is currently made for possible injury to one of the dogs or their handlers, and a large incident may require more dogs.

■ Task forces may need to consider deploying dogs who are specifically trained for cadaver work.

■ Finally, training is everything! Don't rush it. Take the time needed to ensure your dog is truly ready for *all* aspects of a disaster mission.

The New Jersey Task Force was deployed to the World Trade Center for 10 days. Many task force members still can't comprehend the enormity of devastation they encountered at Ground Zero. The team returned to Lakehurst on September 20th for final demobilization and a welcome-home celebration. Since then, the dogs have received countless awards in numerous ceremonies for the work they performed. For handlers, however, the real honor comes from knowing they may have brought closure to a number of bereaved families.

Cadaver Work at the Staten Island Landfill Site (World Trade Center)

Perhaps no mission has yet revealed the difficulty and importance of forensic cadaver work than the terrorist attacks of September 11th, 2001. Truckloads of debris were removed from the World Trade Center and the Pentagon and searched by both humans and dogs.

ARDA handlers were asked to assist in searching tons of debris removed from the World Trade Center and deposited at the Staten Island Landfill. Upon arrival at the site, dog/handler teams were first escorted to a supply tent, where they were outfitted with hazmat suits, safety helmets, rubber examination gloves, work gloves (which they changed every 30 minutes) and a respirator mask. Each handler and dog team was assigned an identification number and given debris piles to work. The handlers were accompanied by helpers carrying buckets to collect any human remains found by the dogs. Each dog team worked 25 to 30 minutes before resting.

The task facing the dog teams was enormous. Truckloads of debris were brought to the landfill day and night. This debris was first transported from the World Trade Center site by barge, then transferred to sanitation trucks for its final journey to the landfill. Once at the landfill, it was deposited in huge piles, where sanitation workers used backhoes to remove the larger pieces of twisted steel. When this task was completed, personnel from various federal agencies went through the

Both humans and dogs were used to search World Trade Center debris that was deposited at the Staten Island Landfill. *Sue Lavoie*

The search for World Trade Center victims at the Staten Island Landfill continued day and night. *Bob Langendoen*

piles with rakes, looking for the aircrafts' black boxes, human remains, personal belongings and other evidence. When raking was completed, the dogs searched the piles. It wasn't uncommon for dogs to indicate the tiny pieces of human tissue or bone that had been missed during the raking process.

Conditions at the landfill added to the difficulty of this mission. Huge sanitation trucks came and went, backhoes moved debris and bulldozers were everywhere. Hundreds of people climbed on and around the piles. Methane gas seeped up from the landfill below. In addition to the distractions from humans and machines, seagulls were attracted to the site. Workers used whistles, rockets and explosions to keep the birds from feeding on the debris. Handlers had to be constantly aware of their surroundings so that they didn't step into the path of an oncoming truck and, obviously, the dogs had to be under complete control to avoid a tragedy.

We can't emphasize enough how important it is to train dogs to search—always under control—in a wide variety of conditions. Dogs need to be able to ignore the noise of large machinery and the scent of bystanders while they search for small human remains.

The search work itself was slow and methodical as the dogs looked for tiny bits of tissue, bone or body fluids. If a handler believed what the dog indicated was human, it was cataloged, placed in a white bucket and taken to the FBI tent, where forensic pathologists verified whether or not it was human tissue or bone.

Handlers found that dogs frequently did not give their trained indications, perhaps because of the overwhelming scent or the number of finds. Dogs trained to give the bark indication instead began to do so out of frustration, which resulted in a rush of rescue workers who expected to find human remains. One dog, trained to bark, began instead to paw and dig when he found tissue, bone or body fluids. He continued with this indication during the several days he worked the site. Other dogs—trained to Sit or Down—could not because there was no room amid the shattered glass, rebar and shards of concrete.

Tissue and body fluids permeated the rubble, which ranged from steel beams to desks and chairs. The dogs alerted on some items of clothing, apparently worn by victims, while ignoring others—perhaps from a store at the World Trade Center. The same applied to shoes—the dogs ignored some shoes while they indicated others. One shoe still contained a victim's foot. The dogs also alerted on sheets of paper that were apparently saturated with body fluids. They found pieces of human tissue the size of a nickel. One dog indicated what appeared to be a wood chip, but which turned out to be a piece of human rib.

When the dogs completed their shifts, they were thoroughly checked by a veterinarian and decontaminated with a bath. Cadaver training aids were available for the dog teams' use, and these enabled the dogs to end their work with a positive experience and a reward.

The events of September 11th, and their aftermath, presented problems and challenges far beyond what most dog teams trained for or ever expected to face—with the exception of the FEMA and state task forces (and even these organizations encountered situations that required their every skill). Whether it is a cadaver dog searching a debris field or a disaster dog searching Ground Zero, the lessons learned from these events will have an impact on search and rescue work for years to come.

This list summarizes observations from handlers who worked at the site:

- For cadaver work, train dogs on all sources (tissue, bone, body fluids, hair, teeth) at various stages of decomposition. While many forensic searches involve older time periods, the landfill experience highlighted the need for training on more recent sources as well.

- As dogs progress in training, add distractions—food, observers and dead animals (roadkill, for example). When you use food as a distraction, make sure the dogs can't reach it to reward themselves. A real mission should *not* be the first time your dog encounters distractions.

- Never forget the basics of reading your dog. The slightest change in body language or behavior might be the only indication you get on a small amount of human scent—the dipped nose, the slight turn of the head, the momentary noticing of *something*. Always check out subtle indications.

- Handle training aids safely, both for your protection and to maintain the integrity of the scent. Training scent should be as pure as possible to ensure that the dogs understand precisely what scent they are expected to indicate.

- Proof dogs to insure they are indicating the cadaver scent rather than, for example, the scent of the container. Use containers with no cadaver material to test the dogs' reactions—as compared to containers that hold cadaver material. If dogs indicate both, go back to training basics until they ignore the empty containers. Also, as stated above, vary training aids so that dogs don't key in on just one scent.

- Keep an accurate log of training materials used, their age and other pertinent details, along with the dog's reaction to each.

- Share your experiences with others. Much of what was encountered on September 11th was new to many teams. It only becomes a learning experience if the information learned is information shared.

- Finally, remember the cardinal rule of all dog handlers: Trust your dog.

Cadaver Search at the Pentagon Debris Field, September 2001

As at the Staten Island Landfill, ARDA handlers who had passed their unit's forensic cadaver certification test were requested to help search for human remains in the debris removed from the Pentagon.

A dog searches debris removed from the Pentagon. *Fairfax County Urban Search and Rescue Team, VA-TFI*

Truckloads of material from the damaged area of the Pentagon were taken to the North Parking Lot and spread out in low piles approximately 20-×-30 yards, with a depth ranging from 4 to 12 feet. The depth varied based on the search stages; the higher piles were hasty-searched by dogs, raked down, searched again, raked again and then given a final sweep with the dogs.

Handlers were outfitted with hazmat suits, rubber gloves, rubber boots and respirator masks before being assigned to search a pile. A "yard boss" directed the handlers to their assigned piles and was responsible for determining which type of search each pile needed—starting with a hasty search, followed by a second pass, and then a third and final sweep. Once the yard boss assigned a handler to a pile, that handler was responsible for conducting the appropriate type of search.

Each pile was spread out first by a front-end loader, then hasty-searched by a dog team. Handlers were allowed no more than 10 minutes for this search. When the dogs finished their initial search, members of various federal agencies raked the pile, looking for remains, evidence and personal belongings. Once this raking was complete, the dog teams made a second sweep. Then more rakers would go through, followed by a final sweep by the dogs. As they made this final sweep, the dogs would work a slower, more methodical search.

Because of the small scent source, dry conditions and high temperatures in the 80s, piles were occasionally watered down with fire hoses to enhance scent and enable the dogs to work with a higher probability of detection.

The dogs' indications varied from a trained Down to much more subtle alerts. Dogs trained to give the Down indication did so some of the time, while at other times they scratched or pawed. Often—due to the small fragments found—an alert was nothing more than the dip of a head or a sharp turn of the nose, as if the dog's head was being jerked with a string.

The remains discovered ranged from pieces the size of a quarter to tissue embedded in metal objects and buried fragments. The dogs indicated all types of human remains, including hair, teeth, bones, skin and cremated bits of tissue.

When the dog indicated a find, his handler was required to signal nearby mortuary workers. Handlers were specifically instructed not to bend down or touch anything. As the workers recovered the remains, the dog/handler teams continued searching other areas of the pile.

The importance of training was shown once again. The site was full of other searchers and heavy machinery, so the dogs had to be under total control. When necessary, handlers used long leashes to provide optimum control and yet allow the dogs to move freely around the pile. Because of the danger on the pile, dogs were rewarded with a strong tug-of-war play session only after they had completed their search and were off the pile. On the pile, handlers often only praised dogs verbally to keep them motivated yet avoided getting them so excited that they would be unable to continue with the slow, methodical search required to locate tiny fragments of human remains. However, some handlers found that failing to reward the dogs sufficiently on the pile led to a rapid loss of motivation. Handlers who face similar situations in the future should keep this in mind and practice a safe—yet motivating—reward system.

Once each dog team finished its assignment, they went to the decontamination tent. Here the dog was bathed and checked thoroughly by a veterinarian. Any clothing the handlers wore over their uniforms was disposed of. Then the teams returned to base camp, where they awaited their next assignment.

ARDA dog teams continued working the site for two weeks, in eight-hour shifts, with literally hundreds of finds.

Oklahoma City Bombing

On a beautiful spring morning in 1995, an explosion shattered the Alfred P. Murrah building in Oklahoma City. More than 100 people died when Timothy McVeigh set off explosives hidden in a rented truck.

Both trained emergency personnel and volunteers in the Oklahoma City area responded to the bombing. They were responsible for saving lives during what is commonly referred to as the Golden 24 Hours—the time when most survivors are found.

FEMA had established its urban search and rescue task force system in the early 1990s, and Oklahoma City was the first major disaster where the full resources of FEMA were implemented. Eleven task forces from around the country responded to the bombing.

ARDA handlers responded with both Maryland Task Force 1 (MD-TF 1) and the Fairfax, Virginia, Task Force 1 (VA-TF 1). The Fairfax, Virginia, Task Force 1 was dispatched from Andrews Air Force Base on April 23, 1995. Upon arrival in Oklahoma City, Task Force 1 was transported to the Myriad Convention Center for a briefing. They were then deployed to a parking garage approximately one block from the Murrah building. The task force had to carry all their equipment—for both search and heavy rescue—from that garage. Task Force members described their first sight of the demolished federal building as "breathtaking."

The search and rescue operation was divided into two 12-hour shifts. The day shift lasted from 7:00 A.M. until 7:00 P.M., and the night shift lasted from 7:00 P.M. through 7:00 A.M. The search itself was conducted under difficult and

A search dog enters a void in the ruins of the Murrah building in Oklahoma City. *Billy Stanton*

dangerous conditions. The Murrah building was in danger of collapsing, and structural engineers had to determine which areas were safe to search and which ones needed shoring before searchers could enter. With the front of the building blown off, both human and canine searchers faced the hazard of working upper floors that had no front walls to prevent them from falling several stories.

Each search team consisted of two search team managers, two technical search specialists (operating the fiber optic cameras and listening devices), and four canine search specialists. Areas where victims had been located were marked with the urban SAR marking system (generally, orange spray paint or tape in symbols that indicated the area had been searched and whether any victims were found). The dogs searched areas after large slabs of concrete had been removed from those areas, and at the beginning of each shift, before the areas were worked by other searchers. The dogs successfully located several bodies and body parts. Technical search specialists were invaluable, as their equipment located a number of victims. This search proved the efficiency of FEMA's multi-resource search system.

As each team finished its shift, it briefed the oncoming team about which areas had been searched and what—if anything—had been found.

FEMA task forces conducted continuous search and rescue operations, 24 hours a day—for more than 13 days. This mission established the viability of the FEMA system, which has proven so successful in recent years.

Earthquake in Izmit, Turkey

On August 17, 1999—at approximately 1:00 a.m. EST—Turkey was devastated by a 7.4-magnitude earthquake. That same day, Task Force 1 of Fairfax, Virginia, was activated by the U.S. Agency for International Development (USAID). This 70-member task force included structural engineers, hazardous material technicians and specialists in heavy rigging, technical information, communications, logistics, medical, and technical and canine search. The team loaded 56,000 pounds of equipment—contained in a tractor-trailer and two smaller trucks—on an Air Force C5. They departed from Dover Air Force Base on August 18th and arrived in Turkey around 2:00 a.m. EST on August 19th.

After a 13-hour flight, the team landed in Istanbul, Turkey. Because of their training—and previous exposure to noise and distractions—all four dogs were content and quiet the entire flight. They arrived in Turkey well-rested, having been allowed to remain in the plane's cabin to sleep. The ladder that unloaded from the aircraft was not the exterior companionway they had used in Dover, but instead a narrow, two-story metal ladder down into the cargo bay. One handler suggested that the dogs must have been eager to relieve themselves, since none of them had any problem with the steep, difficult ladder.

The team was transported by bus to Izmit. The dogs were allowed to ride in the front of the bus—both so they could be boarded last and unloaded first, and to

The destruction caused by a major earthquake is obvious in this picture from Soviet Armenia.
Penny Sullivan

make them as comfortable as possible so they would get to the scene rested and ready to work. The team arrived at 5:30 A.M. local time, unloaded their equipment, and had reconnaissance teams in the field by 6:45 A.M.

The extent of the devastation forced a change in normal shift work, and all available teams began working simultaneously. Due to the critical survival time window, this initial work phase continued for more than 30 hours.

Reconnaissance teams were assigned to search collapsed apartment buildings and homes. Each recon team included two dog/handler teams, a technical search team (using the fiber optic Search Cam and the Delsar listening device), structural engineers, hazmat technicians, medical, and rescue personnel. Since the earthquake struck at 3:00 A.M. local time, search efforts concentrated on sleeping areas. Interpreters assigned to each team provided valuable information about whether someone was inside the structure or not. If there were no people inside, teams did not waste time searching. They moved on to sites where they knew people had been at the time of the quake.

Many buildings had "pancaked" (floors collapsing down on one another), trapping much of the scent. Adding to the difficulty, temperatures hovered around 100° F with very high humidity and little moving air. Voids that had the potential to hold survivors were often 15 to 25 feet below the top of the rubble. This further complicated both scent flow and an ability to effectively search for survivors. At other times, the dogs were the only ones who could work their way up through voids to the top of a row of attached apartments which were partially standing at one end and pancaked at the other. By constantly using all three tools—dogs, fiber optic cameras and listening devices—teams could assess the possibility of life within the rubble. Due to extremely difficult search conditions, close interaction between the technical and canine search teams was invaluable.

As the dogs went about their work, they ignored many distractions—a great deal of noise, dust, automobile traffic and family members awaiting word on their missing relatives.

The dogs' good physical conditioning—gained from constant training, including climbing and crawling—was crucial to their success. The team's medical personnel helped keep the dogs in good shape and able to work throughout their 10-day deployment. Although the sun-heated surfaces—including many brick particles—were hard on the dog's pads, they were able to continue climbing through the rubble. Both dogs and humans were kept continually hydrated, and the dogs occasionally received subcutaneous fluids.

All of the dog's training paid off on this mission. They found one person who was rescued and survived, and another who unfortunately died before the rescue was completed. Including the survivor found by the dogs, the Fairfax team saved four lives in all. Miami's Metro-Dade Task Force (FL-TF 1) relieved Fairfax and continued the search for survivors.

Earthquake in Taiwan

On September 20, 1999, Fairfax Task Force 1 was activated for response to a magnitude 7.6 earthquake in Taiwan. More than 2,000 people were feared dead. Thousands more were missing and believed trapped in the rubble. The Task Force departed Dover, Delaware, aboard a military C5 for the 19-hour, non-stop flight to Taiwan. As soon as the team arrived in Taipei, they had a 3½-hour bus trip to their search sector, which had been assigned by the United Nations On-Site Operations Coordination Center.

Once at their assigned search area, part of the Task Force set up a base of operations on a basketball court outside of a business school, while the other members met with local government officials to help with crisis management and provide information on the Task Force members' capabilities.

While the base was being established, other team members immediately began a reconnaissance of the search sites. The recon team included a search team manager, a hazardous material specialist, a structural specialist, two dog/handler teams, two technical specialists (with fiber optic cameras and listening devices), two rescue specialists and one medical specialist. This team was responsible for mapping the area, determining search priorities and developing information about the sites that would be used to determine future assignments. As the team moved through the area, they systematically worked the dogs. Then handlers assisted the technical specialists with cameras and listening devices, relayed recommendations to the search manager, and moved on to the next site.

The desolation of disaster: An ARDA dog searches for victims of the Mount Saint Helens volcano eruption. *Jeff Doran*

The importance of agility training can be seen during this search for the victims of the Taiwan earthquake in 1999. *Fairfax County Urban Search and Rescue Team, VA-TF1*

Once the reconnaissance was completed, the entire Task Force was split into two shifts, with each shift working 12 hours.

Their first mission was to aid a 32-year-old man trapped in the rubble of a 16-story apartment building in the city of Toulio. His leg was badly entangled and the rescuers planned on amputating it in order to free him. Part of the Task Force's medical team was assigned to help in the rescue and, after eight hours of intense work, managed to free the man without amputating his leg.

This mission presented a unique challenge for the dogs. Most of the assigned sites were apartment buildings completely covered with ceramic tile facades that were coated with a thick layer of concrete dust. Some buildings also had marble or tile on the inside. This combination was extremely slippery for both handlers and dogs. Also, because most of the collapses involved one structure leaning sideways against another, the surface angles were rather extreme, adding to the danger. Makeshift ladders and ropes—and anything else the handlers could find—were laid on the surface to make the work as safe as possible. The importance of agility training was shown once again, as the dogs managed this dangerous situation without injury. The area was also repeatedly struck by strong aftershocks, which kept all Task Force members on their toes while they were working inside the damaged structures.

ARDA units have responded to numerous disaster missions. Here, an ARDA dog searches for flood victims in Johnstown, Pennsylvania in 1977. *Emil Pelcak*

After seven days—their mission complete—the Task Force returned to Taipei. They spent the night in a hotel across from the airport and were surprised by a very powerful aftershock that rocked the hotel and caused an evacuation. Even though many of the emergency stairwells were locked, everyone on the Task Force made it down 20-plus flights of stairs to the parking area—where they discovered that they had been reactivated! A recon team was sent by helicopter to the city of Miencheng, where a 12-story building had collapsed onto the main highway.

Fortunately, the building was evacuated after the first earthquake. The only fatalities at the scene were those unfortunate people on the street. There was nothing the Task Force could do for these victims, so they were demobilized and returned to Taipei for the flight home.

17

First-Aid for Search Dogs

Search missions can be dangerous for both dogs and handlers. Just as handlers must know first aid for humans, they must know how to provide emergency field treatment for their dogs.

Preventive health care is the cornerstone of a long and productive life for your dog. An annual visit to the veterinarian is mandatory, during which the dog must receive a routine physical and any necessary vaccinations. In addition, fecal and blood tests for internal parasites should be performed. Many search dog handlers keep their dogs on heartworm medication year-round as a preventive measure.

In no case should the following first aid information be used to replace veterinary treatment. In all cases, you must seek professional veterinary care as soon as possible.

Protecting Against Tick-Transmitted Diseases

While all dogs must be protected against both internal and external parasites, tick-transmitted diseases—Lyme disease, Rocky Mountain spotted fever, tick paralysis and Ehrlichia deserve special attention.

LYME DISEASE

The primary transmitter of Lyme disease is the common deer tick. Spread of the disease to dogs (or humans) requires that the tick feed for some time on the host animal. Therefore, it is crucial that your dog be checked thoroughly for ticks after being in the woods. Early removal of ticks greatly reduces the risks of a dog contracting this disease. The simplest way to remove a tick is either with your fingers or a tweezers. Slowly and gently pull until the tick is removed. Symptoms of Lyme disease include lameness, joint pain and swelling and possible aggression. Current treatment is with antibiotics, such as tetracycline.

ROCKY MOUNTAIN SPOTTED FEVER

Rocky Mountain spotted fever produces symptoms of depression, high fever, skin hemorrhages and rashes, loss of appetite, joint pain, coma and possible death. Rocky Mountain spotted fever is transmitted by the American dog tick and the wood tick. Tetracycline is used to treat it.

TICK PARALYSIS

Tick paralysis is caused by a toxin released by the tick into the dog's nervous system. This results in symptoms that range from mild unsteadiness to acute immobilization of all four limbs. Removal of the tick should cure this condition.

EHRLICHIA

Ehrlichia is a tick-borne disease that produces lethargy and fever. Joint pain may also occur, but definite diagnosis requires a blood test. Again, tetracycline is used to treat this tick-borne disease.

> To help avoid tick-borne diseases, you should apply a protective dip or spray repellant on your dog—including inside her ears—before you enter the woods.

Emergency First-Aid Care

Health emergencies involving a dog should basically follow human medical guidelines. Search personnel are required to be trained in human first aid and are thus knowledgeable in the ABC's of first-aid care: *A*irway, *B*reathing and *C*irculation. The same priorities also apply to animals.

The cardinal rule of medicine is "Thou shalt do not harm." When treating an injured and frightened animal, this applies to both the dog *and* the handler. Keep in mind that *all dogs bite!* No matter how well you know an injured dog, she should be muzzled—especially if she needs to be carried and is suffering from a painful injury.

The simplest and quickest muzzle is a two-inch wide strip of fabric, cloth, gauze roll, etc., tied around the dog's muzzle with a half-knot on top. Bring the two loose

Step 1: Tie a half-knot over the bridge of the dog's muzzle.

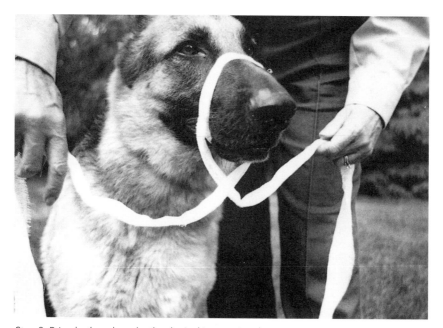

Step 2: Bring both ends under the dog's chin, crossing them.

Step 3: Now bring the crossed ends up on either side of the dog's head behind her ears and tie them securely.

Photo series: *Heidi Ludewig*

KNOW WHAT YOUR DOG'S VITAL SIGNS SHOULD BE

Normal body temperature: 101.5°– 102.5°F (38°– 39°C)
Pulse rate: 70 to 180 beats per minute
Breathing rate: 10 to 30 breaths per minute

ends under the muzzle, cross them and then bring them up behind each ear, tying the ends securely below the crown of the dog's skull. It is a good idea to practice this on your dog when she is healthy, so that the procedure becomes routine.

A word of caution: If the dog is in danger of vomiting or is having difficulty breathing, do not muzzle her.

Since first aid for a dog is about the same as for a human, the following first-aid care is presented in a simplified and brief form. Where there are differences (such as CPR and artificial respiration), a more detailed account will be given. As with any subject, comprehensive articles and books are available for those who want to study canine first aid in greater depth.

Artificial Respiration and CPR

As mentioned previously, you should follow the ABC's of first-aid care. To check for respiration, place your cheek next to the dog's muzzle, *look* for her chest wall rising and falling, and *feel* for the air being exhaled. If you are wearing glasses and your lenses fog, this is a good indication that the dog is breathing.

To perform artificial respiration, you must first clear the airway of debris, fluids, etc. Cup your hands around the dog's mouth, holding her muzzle closed, and blow into her nostrils at a rate of 15 to 20 times per minute. Be sure to allow her lungs to deflate passively for adequate respiratory gas exchange before giving the next breath.

In a situation where mouth-to-nose ventilation is impractical or impossible, an alternative method is as follows. Lay the animal on her right side, extending the head and neck in a straight line with the spine. Pull the tongue forward. Place both hands on the chest wall, slightly forward of the last rib, and compress the chest 12 times per minute.

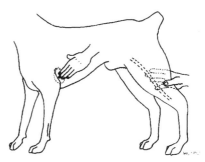

Points for checking a dog's pulse. *Heidi Ludewig*

To check for cardiac function, either feel for a femoral pulse inside the dog's thigh or, with the dog lying on her right side, feel for the heartbeat directly behind and in line with the elbow. If there is no palpable cardiac function, CPR must be initiated.

The heart is most efficiently compressed from side to side in dogs, since this is the narrowest dimension of the thorax. Use a flat, spread hand rather than the heel of your hand. Lay a large dog (one over 25 pounds) on her right side on a hard surface and exert compression over the widest section of the ribcage. (In small dogs, compress the chest wall *between* your two hands, applying compression directly over the heart.) The chest should be compressed at a rate of 80 to 100 compressions per minute. The ratio of respirations to compressions should be about one respiration to every four compressions. Check for a pulse to evaluate the effectiveness of the compressions and check mucous membrane color and refill for adequate oxygenation.

Burns

First aid for burns involves preventing further damage and helping to reduce pain. Prevent your dog from self injury, flush chemical burns, apply cold compresses and—if aid is delayed—apply a dry or saline bandage. Treat your dog for shock.

Diarrhea

The causes of diarrhea are varied, including giardia (a type of protozoa often present in the untreated water search dogs drink), internal parasites, viruses, nerves or digestive insufficiencies. Generally, if the diarrhea lasts only a day or two, restrict or curtail food intake for 24 hours. Follow with a bland diet of chicken or beef with rice to bring the diarrhea under control.

In all other cases of chronic or prolonged diarrhea, get veterinary help to determine the cause. Prolonged bouts of diarrhea can cause severe dehydration and debilitation.

Dislocation

Signs of a dislocation include pain, swelling, abnormal joint function, abnormal joint position or angulation and apparent shortening of the limb. First aid is primarily aimed at keeping the dog as comfortable as possible, since correction of the dislocation usually requires general anesthesia.

Drowning

Unless you can lift your dog and hold her suspended by the hind limbs for 15 to 30 seconds to drain fluid from her lungs, lay her on a sloping surface (with her head lower than the rest of her body) to allow for passive drainage. Check her respiration and cardiac function and begin appropriate first-aid care.

Complications following resuscitation include possible lung damage and infection. The dog should be closely monitored for 48 hours after initial resuscitation at a veterinary hospital to watch for potential problems, including signs of pneumonia.

To reduce the risk of accidental drowning, consider using dog life preservers or tether lines, or removing the dog's collar, depending on the water conditions.

Fractures

Signs of an apparent fracture include pain, swelling, grating (sounds of friction between bone fragments), diminished function, abnormal angulation between joints and abnormal movement. Treatment should prevent further injury and make the dog more comfortable.

When splinting, the objective is to immobilize the break, using any reasonable material (for example, rolled-up newspapers or magazines, wood, cardboard). Pad the break with cotton or cloth, place the splint around the break and secure it with tape, cloth, rope, etc. Immobilize the joints both above and below the fracture site. Another effective splint that will reduce or prevent swelling is a modified Robert Jones bandage (with heavily padded splinting material; see the illustration on page 246).

Frostbite

The clinical signs of frostbite may include redness, paleness or scaliness of the exposed tissues. Treatment involves carefully rewarming the tissues by immersing the area or wrapping it with towels soaked in *lukewarm* water. Never rub or massage a frostbitten area, and be sure to prevent your dog from injuring herself. To protect your dog's feet against frostbite, you may want to apply protective tape bandages or purchase booties.

Gastric Dilation

Commonly—and inappropriately—termed "bloat," this emergency situation arises when the dog's stomach rapidly fills with gas. A further complication is torsion or volvulus, when the stomach or intestines twist. Early symptoms include drooling and salivation, restlessness and pacing, and non-production retching and vomiting. Late-stage symptoms include abdominal distention, difficulty breathing, possibly cyanosis and shock.

First aid involves keeping the animal calm, passing a stomach tube if possible (do not force; there may be torsion) to relieve the distention and transporting the dog to a hospital—*immediately.*

To help prevent gastric dilation, give your dog frequent, small meals instead of one large meal. Don't feed large meals before you begin physical activity. When you're in the field, encourage your dog to take small, frequent drinks rather than filling up all at once.

Heatstroke

Symptoms of heatstroke, or hyperthermia, include elevated temperature, rapid pulse, bright red mucous membranes, weakness, shock and collapse. First aid involves reducing the dog's core temperature as quickly as possible by spraying or immersing the dog in cool water and removing her from the sun and heat. Take the dog's temperature every five minutes and discontinue treatment as soon as it returns to normal, then dry the dog to prevent hypothermia.

The most common cause of hyperthermia is leaving a dog unattended in a closed or only partially ventilated vehicle. On a search mission, dogs may need to be left

When working in hot weather, dogs must be allowed to cool off frequently. *Penny Sullivan*

alone while their handlers are away (for example, during a briefing). We highly recommended that you crate train or tie your dog outside instead of leaving her in a car.

When you are searching, always carry adequate water for both you and your dog and take frequent water breaks. We also recommended that you allow your dog to swim or lie in a stream when she has the opportunity to do so in the field.

Hypothermia

Symptoms of hypothermia include subnormal body temperature, shivering—which discontinues as the dog loses more body heat—decreased pulse rate, weakness, unconsciousness and shock. First aid is aimed at raising the dog's core temperature as quickly as possible. Caution must be used, however, because rewarming too rapidly can induce shock or cardiac arrest.

To rewarm your dog, immerse her in a warm water bath or wrap her in blankets and towels soaked in warm water. If the dog is fully conscious, you can also administer warm liquids. As with hyperthermia, monitor the dog's body temperature and discontinue treatment when her temperature returns to normal. Be careful to avoid burning the dog when you're rewarming her.

Insect Bites and Scorpion Stings

First aid includes removing an insect and/or its stinger, applying cold compresses (or wet compresses of sodium bicarbonate paste, soothing lotion, etc.) and administering an oral antihistamine. In severe reactions, apply ice packs to the affected area. If the bite is on a limb, bandage firmly between the swelling and the body to prevent spread of the toxin and seek professional help immediately.

Open Wounds and Hemorrhage

Open wounds include abrasions, incisions, lacerations and punctures. First aid, in such cases, is to control hemorrhage by using direct pressure/bandage, cold compresses or a constricting band, and to prevent further trauma and/or contamination of the wound. Once bleeding is under control, clean the wound with an antibacterial soap, hydrogen peroxide, or flush with clean water. When bandaging a limb, wrap *from* the extremity *toward* the body.

A constricting band should be applied tightly enough to stop or slow bleeding, but you should still be able to easily slip a finger beneath it. The band should be slowly released for one minute out of every ten, and then retightened only if necessary.

If a true tourniquet needs to be applied to control bleeding (as in complete detachment of a limb or body part), realize that you are risking loss of that limb to

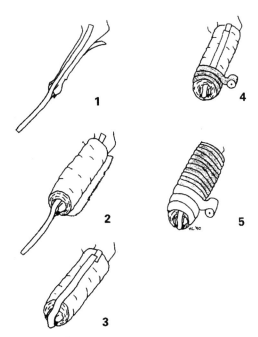

Modified Robert Jones Bandage:

Step 1: Apply two pieces of adhesive tape to the limb, as shown, extending the pieces beyond the toes for a length equal to the length of the limb.

Step 2: Wrap the taped limb in several layers of roll cotton.

Step 3: Bring the tape stirrup over the cotton.

Step 4: Firmly wrap with elastic wrap or gauze bandage, securing the extra tape stirrups to the bandage.

Step 5: Complete by applying adhesive wrap. (Toes are left exposed to facilitate checking limb for circulation). *Heidi Ludewig*

save the life of the dog. Never release a tourniquet once applied, except under orders from a veterinarian (attach a note to the tourniquet recording the time it was applied).

When searching a disaster site where broken glass, wires and other sharp and potentially dangerous rubble abound, it may be advisable to tape the dog's feet. However, the dog will lose some traction and you must weigh the pros and cons of taping or applying booties.

Penetrating Objects

Never remove any object penetrating your dog's eye, chest or abdominal cavity. Leave the object in place, supporting and protecting it with bandage wraps. Protect the site of such wounds from further damage and seek professional help.

If the penetrating object can be removed *safely* and *easily* without hemorrhage and further damage to the tissues, this should be done and the wound should be treated accordingly.

Porcupine Quills: Keep your dog calm to prevent her from pawing at the quills and breaking them off; broken quills cannot be easily removed. If you must remove the quills yourself, grasp the quill close to the skin, then pull slowly and steadily. As the quill moves, readjust your grip close to the skin and continue the slow, steady pull. It's best to get your dog to a veterinarian immediately. She will sedate the dog to remove the quills, and check to ensure that her throat is clear of any quills.

Briers, Foxtails, etc.: Always examine your dog carefully after being out in the field. Thorns, briers, awns, etc., should be removed before they can imbed themselves in the skin and become a potential site for infection. Take care to examine between the toes and paw pads, and inside the ears.

Poisoning

Treatment for poisoning depends upon the toxin ingested. Generally, if the poison was not caustic, induce vomiting by orally administering syrup of ipecac or hydrogen peroxide. If the toxin was caustic or corrosive, do not induce vomiting. Instead, dilute it with milk or vegetable oil mixed with activated charcoal or kaolin. If the poison is a known acid, administer antacids such as milk of magnesia or baking soda. If it is a known alkali (base), administer vinegar or lemon juice.

First aid is primarily meant to reduce the amount of ingested poison that is absorbed by the body. If available, read any labels to find the recommended antidote. Transport the dog immediately to a veterinary hospital, advising the staff in advance of your imminent arrival. Poison control center numbers should be readily available.

Shock

Shock is a life-threatening situation that develops when the body's cells receive inadequate supplies of blood and oxygen. Causes of shock include decreased blood volume due to bleeding, severe stress, infection and/or impaired heart function.

Symptoms of shock are varied. They may include weakness and/or unconsciousness; pale mucous membranes; cool skin and extremities; rapid heart rate;

weak pulse; shallow, rapid breathing; and poor capillary refill (check the capillary refill by pressing down on the gum until it is white, then release pressure to check for an immediate return to pink).

First aid involves maintaining respiration, controlling bleeding, keeping the dog warm, positioning her head slightly lower than her body and monitoring the pulse. In *all* first-aid emergency situations, anticipate shock and be prepared to treat it.

Skunk Odors

Occasionally, search dogs encounter skunks and are sprayed. Remedies for skunk odor include dipping the dog in tomato juice or evenly applying herbal douche to the dog's coat—and then rinsing it off. A product called Outright, produced by the Bramton Company, is also very effective against this problem. Take care to thoroughly flush the sprayed dog's eyes with water. Also, be aware that the dog's searching abilities may be severely affected for several hours.

Snakebites

Although snakebites are rarely fatal, tissue damage can be extensive. Authorities now believe that applying constricting bands or attempting to suck the venom from the wound often does more harm than good. The general consensus at this time regarding first-aid treatment for snakebites is to subdue or immobilize the dog as much as possible. This reduces the uptake of venom into the animal's system. Next, treat the dog for shock and allergic reaction to ensure that her airway remains open, and then transport the dog to a veterinary hospital immediately. If a member of your unit is qualified, intravenous administration of fluids, sedatives and antivenin may be an option.

The severity of snakebite envenomation varies, depending upon the time of year (highest in the spring), the time elapsed since the snake last bit, the age of the snake (young snakes have high peptide fractions), and the aggressiveness and motivation of the snake.

After being bitten by a rattlesnake, this dog is being carried out to slow the uptake of venom. *Penny Sullivan*

Spinal Injuries

The symptoms of a possible spinal injury include pain (which can be severe) in the neck or back, an arched back, reluctance to climb stairs or jump onto an elevated area, weakness, paralysis and/or lack of feeling in the limbs. The objectives of first aid include keeping the dog as immobile as possible, especially in severe cases of spinal trauma where movement might cause spinal cord injury.

The dog should be transported the same way you would transport a human suspected of having spinal cord injury. Maintain the dog's body position and stabilize her neck (a large cervical collar for humans might fit some of the larger search dogs). The dog should be carefully transported on a rigid surface. Remember the ABC's of first-aid care and treat the dog for shock.

First-Aid Kit

The following items should be maintained in a unit's canine first-aid kit, and kept in base camp:

- Activated charcoal

- Adhesive tape

- Antibiotic ointments (topical and eye), sprays, powders and soap

- Bandage scissors

- Cotton-tipped applicators

- Dacriose or other eyewash

- Disposable razors (to clip hair)

- Ear flush

- Elastic bandage (Ace or similar)

- Hydrogen peroxide

- Kwik-Stop styptic powder

- Large butterfly closures

- List of emergency numbers (24-hour veterinarian, poison control centers)

- Milk of magnesia

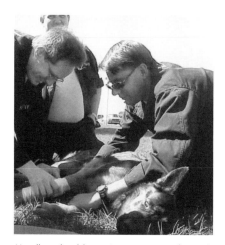

Handlers should practice emergency first-aid procedures. *Joseph Ward, NJ-TF1*

- Nail clippers
- Oral antibiotics
- Oral antihistamines
- Pain relievers (buffered aspirin, Ascription A/D)
- Pepto-Bismol, Kaolin, Kaopectate
- Pliers/wirecutters
- Roll cotton (for cast padding, etc.)
- SAM splint(s)
- Snake antivenom
- Sterile pads/compresses (gauze or Telfa pads)
- Stomach tube
- Thermometer (rectal)
- Tourniquet
- Tranquilizers
- Tweezers/hemostat
- Two-inch bandages (Kling, Webril, Vetrap)

18

ARDA Searches

The following are accounts of some memorable ARDA searches.

Missing Hiker

ARDA's aid was requested in searching for a 20-year-old hiker who had been missing five days and four nights in mountainous terrain. There was little hope of survival. Because other resources had been exhausted during the first four days of the search, only the ARDA unit was left to carry on the search. Arriving too late to search that day, the unit bivouacked at the 7,500-foot level on Mount Adams. Unit members spent the night considering the search and tactics applied, calculating where they thought the subject should be and planning the next day's search.

The following morning, two dog/handler teams were dispatched to the prime area. Within three minutes, the victim was found alive. After five nights and six days, he was suffering from exhaustion and hypothermia. The hiker had traveled a creek drainage off the mountain for six and a half miles. His clothing was badly torn and he had left many of his belongings as he followed the drainage. After an examination—and receiving food and reassurance—he was released to Forest Service headquarters.

Lost Prospector

An ARDA unit was requested to aid in the search for a prospector who was nine days overdue. The sheriff's department had mounted a massive search with no results, and they wanted to use dogs in a last-ditch effort to find the prospector.

The Civil Air Patrol was conducting practice searches when the call was received, making fixed-wing aircraft readily available. An actual mission was declared, allowing two of the aircraft to be used for transporting the dog teams. After arrival and a quick briefing, the handlers and dogs were transported by four-wheel-drive vehicles to the prospector's pickup truck, which was parked on the side of a mountain.

The dog teams were deployed to search the sides of the canyon toward the summit. Approximately four hours into the search, a handler reported a find. Unfortunately, the subject was dead.

The prospector had apparently fallen, broken his leg, tried to stand and had fallen again—this time to his death. Sadly, he had possessed the supplies needed to survive, but he hadn't used them.

Missing Elderly Man

A 76-year-old man was missing from his home in a rural, wooded neighborhood. He was reportedly in good physical condition and took long daily walks of up to several miles. He was last seen by a local resident walking along a road within a quarter mile of his home. The area had been searched by foot, horseback, helicopter and Bloodhounds.

ARDA handlers prepare to board a helicopter for a search that lead to the recovery of an elderly subject, found alive after being lost in the woods for several days. *Emil Pelcak*

Two days after the subject's disappearance, an ARDA unit was requested to join the search. The unit's efforts concentrated on roads, driveways and the areas adjacent to them. Within an hour, a team working a heavily wooded section had an alert. The dog left the handler and moments later returned with an indication of a positive find. Following the dog through heavy brush, the handler heard the subject's voice before she actually saw him.

The man had fallen under barbed wire along an old stone wall, just yards away from a well-used bridle path ridden by searchers that same day, who had failed to see him because of the heavy underbrush. The man spoke to the dog as the handler approached, but lapsed into semiconsciousness due to hypothermia. Members of the Morristown Intensive Care Unit were on scene in minutes, where they stabilized the subject for transport to a local hospital.

A dog alerts on the remains of a homicide victim buried in a landfill for nearly one year. *Penny Sullivan*

Homicide

The state police requested the aid of an ARDA unit to locate the body of a man who had been missing and presumed dead for four months. The problem presented by the time lapse was compounded by the terrain, which included a semiarid area near a river where only scant moisture had fallen since the victim had disappeared.

The unit began their search at the intersection of a highway and a dirt road, which was the most likely the point last seen. In a very short time, one of the dogs alerted on an area approximately 75 yards from base camp. The other two handlers responded to that site where—as if on signal—all three dogs began to dig and whine. Authorities started digging and discovered the subject's left foot at a depth of about 18 inches.

The search served as a reminder that all searches should begin at the base camp boundaries, not a half mile down the road!

Missing Deaf Woman

ARDA was requested to assist in searching for a 72-year-old woman who was deaf, mute and diabetic. She had last been seen behind her house at 4:00 the previous afternoon, heading into the woods to find her husband, who had gone to chop wood.

Three dog/handler teams and a base operator responded and, after the initial interviews and a review of the map, began searching the woods and the maze of logging trails around the woman's house.

One handler had nearly completed his sector when his dog made a pronounced alert but lost the scent near the sector boundary. The handler finished his sector and radioed base that he was going to conduct a hasty search of a logging road beyond the sector boundary and in the general area of the alert. As he walked along the road, the handler saw his dog in the distance, approaching what appeared to be a large stump. When he got closer, however, he realized that the top part of the "stump" was the woman, sitting and tapping her walking stick. Through sign language, she let her rescuers know that she had been walking in circles and wanted to go home. Despite being diabetic and spending the night in the woods, she was in good shape and was able to walk back to her house.

Skeletal Remains

This incident was not a search, but a unit workout. A light brush problem was planned for a unit trainee. As it was her first long problem, an experienced handler went along to provide guidance. In addition, the trainee's mother was visiting from California and she, too, was trudging along behind as the dog started to work on the Find command.

The problem was going very well when, after about 45 minutes, the dog gave an alert. At first the object indicated by the dog did not look like anything special, just a stick on the ground. As the unit members approached, however, it took on definite form. The dog had alerted on a human skull with what appeared to be a bullet hole in the back of the head.

The authorities were notified and, upon their arrival, the area was roped off. At the request of the FBI, the unit returned to the site and subsequently found leg and pelvic bones. The body parts were identified as having come from four different individuals, all homicide victims.

This find pointed out two things: Don't consider all workouts to be routine, and you should check out every alert your dog gives. You never know what you'll find.

A joyful ending to an ARDA search for a young boy. *Tony Campion*

Lost Child

ARDA's assistance was requested in the search for a missing two-year-old child who had disappeared along with his three dogs.

Two dog/handler teams responded immediately, with a third scheduled to respond as soon as possible. The two handlers began a hasty search of the roads and paths around the boy's home. They met at an abandoned railroad line, where they found a sandy area containing small footprints and dog tracks. The two handlers split up, with each handler walking in a different direction along the railroad line in an attempt to find more tracks.

The third handler arrived, and one of the handlers walking along the railroad noticed the bright orange parka in the distance as that handler walked to meet him. At the same time, he noticed a brown flash cross the tracks between him and the other handler. The animal appeared too small and dark to be a deer, so he assumed it was one of the child's dogs. The handler continued toward that point, which was in the middle of a large swampy area that looked difficult for a small boy to cross.

When the handler reached the point where he had seen the animal cross the rail line, he took his dog into the woods, wading through water that averaged around six inches deep. As he walked he called the child's name—and was surprised to hear a feeble answer. The railroad had been upwind of this side of the woods. But when the child answered, the dog also alerted and led the handler to the boy. He

A dog indicates the stone wall where the body of a homicide victim was found buried. *Penny Sullivan*

was soaking wet, wearing a stocking cap pulled down over his eyes, and sobbing and asking for his mother. He was more than a mile from home.

Homicide

ARDA was requested to search an area near Cairo, New York, for a female employee of IBM who was feared to be a homicide victim. The woman had last been seen leaving work two weeks earlier. A man wanted in connection with the murder of a Westchester County police officer had been arrested in Toronto, Canada, driving the missing woman's car. A woman's scalp was found in the car.

As a result, a search was initiated in a New York area frequented by the suspect. This search led to a burglarized cabin that contained property belonging to the suspect and the missing woman's IBM identification card.

The area around the cabin was searched by police, forest rangers and volunteers for one week without success. The ARDA unit was asked to search the same area and responded with two dog/handler teams.

Despite snow flurries and high winds, one of the dogs made a strong alert and led his handler to a stone wall. Although it seemed impossible for a body to be hidden in the wall, the handler had strong faith in his dog's reliability and police were called to the scene. Removal of the stones did indeed reveal the scalped body of the missing woman. The suspect had apparently used her scalp as a wig to disguise himself when he crossed the Canadian border. The suspect was later killed by police as he attempted to escape.

Appalachian Trail Murders

A young man and woman hiking the Appalachian Trail were reported 10 days overdue. An ARDA unit was requested to assist in searching for the hikers, responding with four dog teams and a base operator.

The search area encompassed 32 miles of the trail. Resources included mounted searchers, members of six different rescue squads, the local sheriff's department, state police and Forest Service personnel.

The dogs began working several miles of trail north of the point where the hikers were last seen. Early that evening, another hiker reported that he had found the female subject's body, in a sleeping bag hidden under leaves near a shelter north of the original search area. The woman's body was removed, the area sealed off and search efforts suspended until the following morning.

The next morning, three dogs worked the trail leading to the shelter. A fourth dog was brought to the site where the woman's body had been found in an effort to locate evidence. While searching near the body site, the dog gave a pronounced alert and led her handler to a wooded hillside more than 100 feet away. The dog's strong alert—and the sight of a freshly broken branch at the base of the hill— caused the handler to ask for accompaniment from the investigating team before proceeding up the hill.

A short time after their arrival, the dog indicated a large log at the top of the hill. The male subject's body was found behind it, also in a sleeping bag and covered

A dog alerts in a pile of logs left in the wake of the Mount Saint Helens eruption. *Jeff Doran*

with logs and leaves. Both subjects had been dead approximately 10 days. The woman had been stabbed repeatedly and the man had been shot in the head three times. Their murderer was arrested and convicted of the crime.

Missing Child

ARDA was asked to dispatch teams on a search for a two-year-old child. The child had wandered away from his family's mobile home at 5:00 P.M. the previous evening, and he had not been seen since. Because of the cold night temperatures and terrain, dog teams were dispatched on an emergency basis.

Four dog/handler teams began searching with the assistance of man trackers as they attempted to determine a direction of travel. Each dog team worked approximately 150 yards ahead of their respective trackers. About an hour and a half into the search on the second morning, a unit dog alerted and led his handler to the child. He was lying face down in frozen mud behind a log, nearly a mile beyond what was described as an "impassable" fence.

The child did not move, even when the handler called out to him. As the handler leaned over and touched the apparently lifeless body, the boy suddenly whirled and wrapped his arms around the handler's neck. He did not release his grip during the helicopter evacuation and only relinquished his hold when he was reunited with his parents. Doctors said that the boy was within three or four hours of death when he was found. Fortunately, he fully recovered from his ordeal.

Lost Hiker

ARDA was requested to assist on a search for a hiker who had been missing for three months. A large search had been conducted shortly after the man's disappearance, but was suspended due to deep snow and avalanche danger.

Three dog/handler teams responded to the request and began working their sectors. As the dogs worked, a news helicopter flew over. One of the dogs promptly alerted as the downdraft from the helicopter stirred up air currents. The three dogs continued working, a and short time later, one dog working higher on the canyon wall also alerted. Shortly afterward, the third dog also alerted and moved uphill to find the hiker's body. The total time elapsed for the search was less than two hours.

Lost Boy

An ARDA unit responded to a search for a missing three-year-old boy. He had last been seen playing in his yard, which was surrounded by forest.

Following the initial interview and unit briefing, dog teams began hasty searches along probable escape or funneling routes. Sector searching began at 11:00 that night, with dogs and handlers working through dense, marshy terrain.

Shortly after 1:00 A.M., the search was suspended for the night. One handler decided to finish her sector before she returned to base. As she moved upslope near a natural gas pipeline, her dog alerted. At the same time, they heard a dog barking and moved in the direction of both the search dog's alert and the barking dog. As the handler flashed her light into the brush, she caught sight of a shiny blonde object under a pine tree. It was the hair of the little boy, who was hiding and shivering uncontrollably. Transported home, he recovered from his 10 hours of being lost in the woods.

Missing Teenager

A young man joined his friends for a party in the woods in an area aptly known as the Devil's Den. A local resident, hearing the party in progress, called the police. When the police arrived, the young man apparently panicked and ran into the woods. In the dark, he failed to see a cliff in front of him, and he fell over the edge.

An ARDA unit was called in two days later to help search for him. One team started hasty searches soon after they arrived, working in extremely difficult night search conditions. These conditions included steep, tangled terrain that was surrounded by cliffs.

The dog being used was trained to give a bark alert on finding live subjects. As the handler and her radio operator were working their way down a chute next to the rock face, they heard the dog begin barking below them. He continued barking as the handler carefully worked her way down through dense brush to his side.

The dog was standing over the young man's body, which was approximately 100 feet from the base of the cliff, where he had apparently crawled. The subject had suffered multiple skull fractures and was unconscious, with a slow pulse. The handler called for medical evacuation and—although he spent almost a month in the hospital—the young man was expected to make a full recovery.

Missing Snowmobilers

In an apparent attempt to take a shortcut, two snowmobilers drove their vehicles across a forbidden area of ice where aerators kept patches of ice open to avoid fishkills. Both vehicles crashed through the ice and the drivers disappeared. One body was recovered shortly after the accident, but wind pushed the second body under the ice.

Although the ice was 10 inches thick in places and the temperature hovered at 15°F, an ARDA unit was called to assist in the search. During the first day's search, a glove identified as belonging to one of the snowmobilers was found.

A man meets the ARDA dog who found him.
Penny Sullivan

However, the second body was not recovered.

On the second day of the search, ARDA dogs worked the ice pack itself—on lead for safety reasons. One of the dogs gave an indication at a pressure crack in the ice, some distance from where the snowmobilers had disappeared. Because officials thought the area was not a logical place, based on its distance from the accident, no effort was made to put divers in the water at that point. The next day, the official search was suspended, but the family hired a private company and divers to continue the effort. Several days later, they found the second body near the area of the dog's alert.

Missing Woman

A young woman in her 30s was reported missing by her husband. She had left their home at approximately 4:00 P.M. to look for a Christmas tree in the nearby woods, and was overdue. Although the temperatures were below zero and snow was falling, the woman's husband reported that his wife was healthy, and was wearing appropriate clothing for the northern cold. She was also accompanied by her two dogs. After local authorities searched the house and its surroundings, they requested the assistance of an ARDA unit. The unit responded with seven search dog teams, all of which were deployed at 1:00 A.M.

The subject reported that she knew her rescue was imminent when she saw the green lightstick attached to a dog's collar bobbing toward her at 4:30 A.M. The dog gave her a "comforting wet kiss" before returning to his handler on a refind.

A member of this ARDA unit met the subject later, and the subject's words remind all dog handlers why they spend so many hours training to work in all types of weather and terrain. Although her words are paraphrased here, they are still revealing:

> Do you know how dark it gets at night when you are scared, cold and alone? Do you know just how scary it is when you think you might die, on your own land, and die all alone? Well, I do. I have nightmares sometimes from my experience. But then there was a light

A dog finds a young boy. *Penny Sullivan*

bobbing in the woods. The next thing I knew, I was getting sloppy kisses from a huge German Shepherd who I have never seen before. Following her were two men with backpacks and radios. I have never been so happy than I was at that time. The searchers took care of me and got me home safely. I can't tell them how thankful I am for that. My Christmas would have been very different if it wasn't for that dog.

This is why you are training a dog, and why we wrote this book.

Lost Person
Behavior

The following are lost-person statistics (distance found from point last seen) as contained in Analysis of Lost Person Behavior: An Aid to Search Planning, *by William G. Syrotuck (Arner Publications, 1976). The statistics were based on a total of 229 cases, broken down by state as follows: 117 from Washington, 95 from New York and 17 from the states of Idaho, Oregon, California, Alaska, New Mexico, Wyoming and Tennessee.*

This study did not include extremely mountainous terrain, such as the Rocky Mountains, or desert areas. It primarily pertained to forested areas with level to moderately steep terrain. Each unit must determine their own statistics based on the case histories of their region.

CATEGORY BREAKDOWNS

SMALL CHILDREN (ONE TO SIX YEARS OF AGE, 22 CASES)

Toddlers (ages one to three)

Toddlers are usually drawn away by random incidents, such as the appearance of an animal. Sometimes they follow a path for the sheer joy of it. Toddlers are unaware of the concept of being lost and may travel for hours before deciding "I want my mommy," or before they feel alone, tired or hungry. They are likely to remain in the general area and find the handiest place to fall asleep.

Children (ages three to six)

These children are more mobile and have definite interests: finding a playmate, exploring or following older children around. They do have a concept of being lost and usually will make an effort to find a sleeping spot for the night.

> **The case studies revealed:**
>
> Used travel aids: 57 percent. (This percentage used paths, game trails or followed a drainage that afforded a path of least resistance. The remaining 43 percent were found in brushy areas.)
>
> Distances found: within one mile, 38 percent; between one and two miles, 46 percent; between two and three miles, 8 percent; beyond three miles, 8 percent.

CHILDREN (SIX TO TWELVE YEARS OF AGE, 24 CASES)

These children have better navigational and distance skills than younger children, so they are usually well-oriented to their normal surroundings. They may wander off to sulk, gain attention or avoid impending punishment. Once discovering they are lost, they may be profoundly embarrassed or fearful of being punished. At the outset, they may be unwilling to answer calls. However, with darkness, cold or other fears, they are usually happy to help themselves be found.

> **The case studies revealed:**
>
> Used travel aids: 67 percent.
>
> Distances found: within one mile, 33 percent; between one and two miles, 42 percent; between two and three miles, 17 percent; beyond three miles, 8 percent.

HUNTERS (100 CASES)

The nature of hunting is such that hunters tend to concentrate more on game than on navigation. The more isolated and rugged the terrain, the greater the likelihood of getting lost.

> **The case studies revealed:**
>
> Used travel aids: 52 percent; the remaining 48 percent were located in timbered or heavily vegetated areas.
>
> Distances found: within one mile, 18 percent; between one and two miles, 47 percent; between two and three miles, 24 percent; beyond three miles, 11 percent.

HIKERS (44 CASES)

Hikers usually rely on trails and have some destination in mind. Many hikers who become lost have inadequate maps or none at all and run into problems when trail conditions change. Other hikers get lost when they are mismatched with their companions in terms of skills and experience, resulting in their being left behind and separated from the party.

The case studies revealed:

Used travel aids: 73 percent. Hikers tend to use the path of least resistance

Distances found: within one mile, 25 percent; between one and two miles, 25 percent; between two and three miles, 25 percent; beyond three miles, 25 percent.

MISCELLANEOUS OUTDOOR PERSONS (15 CASES)

These comprise a miscellany—mainly adult—of pine cone seekers, berry pickers, mushroom pickers, rock hounds, nature photographers, and others. Generally, people in this category intend to stay near a road or one particular location. Because their plans are short-term, they don't carry any navigational or survival aids. They generally start in good weather and seldom carry spare sweaters or rain gear.

The case studies revealed:

Used travel aids: 30 percent; 10 percent were found in the terrain that occupied their activities.

Distances found: within one mile, 22 percent; between one and two miles, 41 percent; between two and three miles, 11 percent; beyond three miles, 23 percent.

ELDERLY PERSONS (ABOVE 65 YEARS OF AGE, 24 CASES)

Older persons who are senile or suffering from Alzheimer's disease often pose the same supervision problem as small children. They are easily attracted to things that strike their fancy. Active senior citizens are likely to overextend themselves and have a heart attack or suffer from exhaustion—with a fatal outcome.

The case studies revealed:

Used travel aids: 47 percent.

Distances found: within one mile, 57 percent; between one and two miles, 28 percent; between two and three miles, 8 percent; beyond three miles, 7 percent.

Index

A

Accepting people test, 44

Accuracy, response to search and, 137–139

Acetaminophen, 92

Active indication training, cadaver training, 187–191

Adults, 105

Advanced cadaver training, 185–187

Advanced search training, 73–87
 adjusting to dog's working pace, 74–75
 finding unconscious victim, 78–80
 improving search skills, 73–78
 problem solving, 86–87
 testing and polishing search skills, 80–86

Agency personnel, response to search and, 138–139

Aggressive dogs, 29–30

Agility, disaster training and, 201–203

Agility obstacles
 culvert pipes, 49
 55-gallon oil drums, 47
 jumps, 47–49
 ladders, 49
 platforms, 49
 ramps, 47
 teeter-totters, 49
 training, 46–50

Air Force Rescue and Recovery Service, Scott Air Force Base, Illinois, 5

Air scenting, 2–4
 German Shepherd Dog's ability, 2
 tracking to, 2–3

Air-scenting search dog selection, 17–32
 scent theory, 22–27
 search dogs *versus* tracking dogs, 17–21

Alerting, avalanche training, 172

Allergy kits, 92

Amateur radios, 97

American Kennel Club (AKC), 1

American Rescue Dog Association (ARDA), 3, 6
 formation of, 1–10
 German Shepherd Dogs and, 27–28
 handler standards (*See* handler standards)
 naming, 6–7

American Rescue Dog Association (ARDA) searches, 251–261
 Appalachian Trail murders, 257–258
 homicide, 253, 256
 lost boy, 258–259
 lost child, 255–256
 lost hiker, 258
 lost prospector, 251–252
 missing child, 258
 missing deaf woman, 254
 missing elderly man, 252–253
 missing hiker, 251
 missing snowmobilers, 259–260
 missing teenager, 259
 missing woman, 260–261
 skeletal remains, 254

Analysis of Lost Person Behavior, 9, 263

Appalachian Trail murders, ARDA search, 257–258

Area research on search, 107–108

Article searching, 162

Artificial respiration for dogs, 241–242

Aspirin, 92

Attitude of trainer, 14

Avalanche training, 8, 167–175
 alerting and dispatching, 172
 dog indications, 173–174
 group practice sessions, 171
 at night, 174–175